family fun **or** fun for one!

the family
book of
bible fun

Randy Petersen

TYNDALE HOUSE PUBLISHERS, INC.
WHEATON, ILLINOIS

Visit Tyndale's exciting Web site at www.tyndale.com

Some material in this Book was previously published in "The Family Book of Bible Fun,"
and "The Complete Book of Bible Puzzles," vols. 1 and 2.

Edited by Rick Blanchette
Designed by Justin Ahrens
Typeset by Joyce Svensen

ISBN 0-7394-0812-7

Printed in the United States of America

Dedication

*I'd like to dedicate this book to
Mom and Dad,
who taught me the Bible
and lived it out
in ways that have brought me
much joy.*

CONTENTS

Acknowledgments

Many thanks to Deb Austin, assistant and researcher for this book. She contributed many of the ideas, puzzles, and mazes.

Thanks to Cynthia Johnson McBrayer for her fine work on the drawings; to Robin Yeager and Myrna Grolnick for their brilliant activity ideas; to Ken Petersen for the idea; and to Rick Blanchette, my editor, for nursing it along. I also appreciate the assistance of the Tyndale House staff and the Hope Church drama group for being our "studio audience" for the "Feud" material.

INTRODUCTION

"They just don't pay attention! I can't find anything that will keep them interested."

I was talking with a friend who had grade-school children. He was bemoaning his failed attempts at "family devotions." They tried to set aside daily times of prayer and Bible reading, but the kids were bored by it. The pain was etched on his face as he told me this.

That's a sad reality for many families. When they crack open the Bible, the kids get cranky.

It was different in my home as I was growing up. To be honest, we never did much with an organized family devotional time. But every Sunday afternoon, Dad pulled out a Bible quiz book, and we played games. With this weekly activity, my brother, sister, and I learned facts about the Bible.

Facts are just facts. They don't necessarily create a deep faith. But as I learned the names and places of the Bible, I felt at home in this book. The Bible became a rich storehouse of wonderful stories, great people, and strange events. More than anything, I learned that the Bible could be *fun*.

Mom and Dad did more than just emcee the Bible quizzes. They modeled Christianity in their lives. They talked at the dinner table about how we could live in ways that pleased Christ. They regularly asked us about what we were learning in Sunday school and youth group. The quizzes were just threads in the fabric of Christian upbringing. But they helped.

I want to share some of this fun with you. This book is chock-full of quizzes, games, and activities for your whole family or for individual family members. I hope it can be part of your family fabric, too.

Part One

family fun

Section 1

quizzes

MULTIPLE CHOICE

■

Notes on Quiz Giving

In family situations, you will need one person to be a "quizmaster"—someone who can read the questions clearly and check the answers. You may also want a separate scorekeeper, someone who can tally points faithfully. Before you begin, decide what *format* you will follow and what *multilevel arrangements* you might observe.

Format: If you have participants of about the same ability and quickness, try a *free-for-all*. That is, the first person to shout out the correct answer gets the point. Or, you might want to try the *buzzer* system. The best way to play this is to give each person a different word to say, perhaps a different color or even his or her own name. The first person to say his or her word gets the right to answer the question and has 10 seconds to give the right answer. Give two points for a right answer, but take away one point for a wrong answer or a no-answer, and give the next question to the others in the group.

If you have people of very different ages or abilities, play the *round-robin* method. Each person gets a turn to answer a question on his or her own.

Multilevel arrangements: Some of the quizzes offered here are multiple choice. To make them harder, just ask the question without any of the multiple choice answers. To make them easier, allow the person to use a Bible to look up the answer. So if you are playing with Whiz-kid Willy who's 14, Average Alice who's 10, and Slow Sam who's 7—play a buzzer or round-robin format. Give Willy just the questions, without the choices; give Alice the choices; and let Sam use a Bible. That should even things out.

You might also adjust the scoring so that younger ones get more points for each right answer. Or, the person in last place (whoever it may be at the time) gets three points for a right answer, and the person in next-to-last place gets two. This isn't cheating; it's just a way to keep the game fun for everyone.

MULTIPLE CHOICE

1

Goin' Down to da Feet

1. Why was Moses told to take off his sandals in front of the burning bush (Exod. 3:5)?
   a. His feet were sore from climbing Mount Sinai.
   b. It was holy ground.
   c. The sandals were made of Egyptian material.
   d. The sandals would melt from the heat.

2. While Jesus was having dinner in someone's home, a woman washed his feet with her tears and wiped them with her hair. What did she pour on Jesus' feet (Luke 7:38)?
   a. Olive oil
   b. Perfume
   c. Water from the Jordan River
   d. Foot powder

3. Who told Jesus, "No, you shall never wash my feet" (John 13:8)?
   a. Judas
   b. Satan
   c. Peter
   d. John the Baptist

4. Finish this sentence: "Heaven is my throne, and the earth is my ____" (Isa. 66:1).
   a. courtyard
   b. carpet
   c. sandal
   d. footstool

5. According to Ephesians 1:22, what has God put under Christ's feet?
   a. Sin
   b. The earth
   c. Shoes of gold
   d. All things

6. Finish this sentence about the unrighteous, from Romans 3:15: "Their feet are swift to shed ____."
   a. blood
   b. their shoes
   c. the path
   d. toenails

7. Who said he was not even worthy to carry Jesus' sandals?
   a. Judas
   b. Satan
   c. Peter
   d. John the Baptist

8. The king of Babylon had a dream, which Daniel interpreted. In the dream he saw a statue with a head of gold and a chest of silver. What were the feet made of (Dan. 2:33)?
   a. Bronze
   b. Iron
   c. Clay
   d. Iron and clay

9. In Acts 3:8, we read of a man who was "walking and jumping, and praising God," shortly after meeting with Peter and John. Why was he doing this?
   a. He had just heard about Jesus' resurrection.
   b. He had been lame but had just been healed.
   c. He was a beggar, and they had just given him a great amount of gold.
   d. He once was blind, but now he could see.

10. According to Isaiah 52:7, whose feet are "beautiful"?
    a. Angels'
    b. Isaiah's
    c. Those who walk in the temple courts
    d. Those who bring good news

MULTIPLE CHOICE

2

Just Kidding (Sons and Daughters)

1. Dinah had lots of brothers. But who was her father?
   a. Jacob
   b. Jesse
   c. David
   d. Saul

2. In Matthew 8:14-15, we read of Jesus healing a woman of a fever. We don't know her name, but we know her famous son-in-law. Who was he?
   a. James
   b. Peter
   c. Andrew
   d. John the Baptist

3. Zechariah was speechless after he learned he was going to have a son. Who was his famous son?
   a. James
   b. Peter
   c. Daniel
   d. John the Baptist

4. Isaac had two sons. One was nicknamed "Edom"; who was the other one?
   a. Joseph
   b. Jacob
   c. Esau
   d. Ishmael

5. What early church leader was known as the "Son of Encouragement" (Acts 4:36)?
   a. Paul
   b. Peter
   c. Barnabas
   d. Apollos

6. Amram and Jochebed had three children who figured prominently in the history of Israel. Who were these kids?
   a. Shem, Ham, and Japheth
   b. Miriam, Moses, and Aaron
   c. Shadrach, Meshach, and Abednego
   d. Joel, Amos, and Obadiah

7. The servant-woman Hagar tried to run away from home while she was pregnant with her son, Ishmael. Who was Ishmael's dad?
   a. Noah
   b. Abraham
   c. Isaac
   d. Jacob

8. Finish this prophecy about the coming Messiah, from Isaiah 9:6: "For to us a child is born, to us ____."
   a. a Wonderful Counselor appears
   b. a babe in a manger comes
   c. a son is given
   d. a virgin will conceive

9. Naomi had two daughters-in-law. Who were they?
   a. Miriam and Rahab
   b. Miriam and Ruth
   c. Orpah and Ruth
   d. Rahab and Orpah

10. According to a prophecy quoted in Acts 2:17, "Your sons and daughters will prophesy." Who preached the sermon quoting this text?
    a. Peter
    b. Paul
    c. Matthias
    d. Jesus

MULTIPLE CHOICE

3

Pigging Out

1. What church did Paul criticize for "pigging out" on food and wine at the Lord's Supper?
   a. The Romans
   b. The Corinthians
   c. The Ephesians
   d. The Athenians

2. According to Matthew 8:28-34, what happened when some demons asked Jesus to cast them into a herd of pigs?
   a. He did, and the pigs ran down the hill into the sea.
   b. He did, and the pigs began foaming at the mouth.
   c. He refused to do this because pigs were "too good" for these demons.
   d. He cast them into the greedy pig herders instead.

3. Who ate their fill and had 12 baskets of food left over?
   a. The disciples at the Last Supper
   b. The lepers healed by Jesus
   c. The 5,000 Jesus fed with five loaves and two fish
   d. The Israelites eating manna in the wilderness

4. Who got a job tending pigs and got so hungry that he wished he could eat the pods that he was feeding them?
   a. Moses
   b. David
   c. The Prodigal Son
   d. The poor man at the rich man's gate

5. In Philippians 3:19, Paul criticized the greedy enemies of the gospel. What did he say was their "god"?
   a. Their pleasure
   b. Their wine
   c. Their stomach
   d. Their pride

6. According to Jesus' teaching, what are you not supposed to throw to pigs?
   a. Olive branches
   b. Pieces of silver
   c. Pearls
   d. New wine

7. Fill in the following blanks from 2 Thessalonians 3:10: "If a man will not ____, he shall not ____."
   a. eat . . . live
   b. work . . . eat
   c. love . . . live
   d. cook . . . eat

8. Who saw a sheet coming down from heaven with all sorts of forbidden food on it?
   a. Peter
   b. Paul
   c. Jesus
   d. Aaron

9. According to Matthew 11:19, who was called "a glutton and a drunkard, a friend of tax collectors and 'sinners'"?
   a. Herod
   b. Pilate
   c. John the Baptist
   d. Jesus

10. Who ate the scroll God gave him and found it "sweet as honey"?
    a. Isaiah
    b. Ezekiel
    c. Malachi
    d. Paul

MULTIPLE CHOICE

4

Fast Forward

1. Who "hurried off and found Mary and Joseph, and the baby, who was lying in a manger"?
   a. The shepherds
   b. The wise men
   c. Herod's soldiers
   d. The angels

2. According to Ecclesiastes 1:5, what "hurries back to where it rises"?
   a. A wave of the sea
   b. The Babylonian army
   c. The sun
   d. The young lion

3. Who said, "Quick! Let me have some of that red stew! I'm famished"?
   a. Elisha
   b. Elijah
   c. Ezra
   d. Esau

4. According to 1 Kings 11:2, "Nevertheless, Solomon held fast to them in love." Who or what was Solomon "holding fast" to?
   a. His thousand wives and concubines
   b. His great riches
   c. The priests God had appointed
   d. God's commands

5. What does the book of Proverbs call the person who is "quick to quarrel" (Prov. 20:3)?
   a. A sluggard
   b. A fool
   c. An ant
   d. A rabble-rouser

6. Who was upset when Nineveh proclaimed a fast?
   a. King Hezekiah
   b. The prophet Amos
   c. Assyrian king Tiglath-Pileser
   d. The prophet Jonah

7. The king of Babylon looked for young men who were "well informed, quick to understand, and qualified to serve in the king's palace." Name one of the men he found.
   a. David
   b. Daniel
   c. Samson
   d. Shadrach

8. At one point, Jonathan gave this message to David: "Hurry! Go quickly! Don't stop!" Why?
   a. David had insulted Jonathan.
   b. Jonathan's father was trying to kill David.
   c. The Israelite army was heading out to fight the Philistines.
   d. Goliath was getting away.

9. Who said to Peter, "Quick! Get up!" and removed chains from his wrists?
   a. Rhoda
   b. John
   c. The Philippian jailer
   d. An angel

10. Who was told, "Hurry! Take your wife and your two daughters who are here, or you will be swept away when the city is punished"?
    a. Rahab's husband
    b. Abraham
    c. Lot
    d. Achan

MULTIPLE CHOICE

5

Give Me a Hand

1. In what book do we read, "In his right hand he held seven stars"?
   a. Genesis
   b. Job
   c. Daniel
   d. Revelation

2. Who was told, "Do not lay a hand on the boy. . . . Now I know that you fear God, because you have not withheld from me your son"?
   a. Adam
   b. Abraham
   c. Jacob
   d. David

3. Who was born with his hand grasping his brother's heel?
   a. Cain
   b. Jacob
   c. Aaron
   d. Andrew

4. Who said, "Unless I . . . put my finger where the nails were, and put my hand into his side, I will not believe it"?
   a. Abraham
   b. Simon the Pharisee
   c. Thomas
   d. Judas

5. In the midst of a dry spell, Elijah's servant saw something "as small as a man's hand" rising from the sea. What did he see?
   a. A bird
   b. A great fish
   c. A cloud
   d. An angel

6. Who interpreted the handwriting on the wall?
   a. Joseph
   b. Nathan
   c. Daniel
   d. Simon the Sorcerer

7. According to Jesus, what are you not supposed to let your left hand know (Matt. 6:3)?
   a. What your right hand is doing
   b. How to dishonor God
   c. What time it is
   d. The price of spring wheat

8. Who "dipped his hand into the bowl" with Jesus at the Last Supper (Matt. 26:23-25)?
   a. John
   b. Peter
   c. Mary
   d. Judas

9. Why were the Pharisees upset when Jesus healed a man with a shriveled hand (Mark 3:1-6)?
   a. He did this on the day of rest.
   b. He did not wash his hands first.
   c. He did not heal all the crippled people.
   d. They wanted to heal the man first.

10. In Nehemiah 4:17, it says, "Those who carried materials did their work with one hand and held a weapon in the other." What were these materials for?
   a. The ark
   b. The governor's new house in Jericho
   c. Catapults for the battle against the Babylonians
   d. The wall of Jerusalem

MULTIPLE CHOICE

6

Red All Over

1. What biblical hunter was given the nickname Edom, which means "Red"?
   a. Nimrod
   b. Ishmael
   c. Esau
   d. Goliath

2. To whom did Roman soldiers give a scarlet robe and say, "Hail, king of the Jews"?
   a. Hezekiah
   b. Herod
   c. Caesar Augustus
   d. Jesus

3. Who led the Israelite women in a tambourine songfest on the shores of the Red Sea?
   a. Moses
   b. Aaron
   c. Miriam
   d. Deborah

4. In Revelation 6, John saw four horses, representing future destruction. One was red, another was "pale." What were the colors of the other two horses?
   a. Black and white
   b. Both were brown
   c. Blue and gray
   d. One was spotted, the other striped

5. What structure had a ceiling of "ram skins dyed red"?
   a. Noah's ark
   b. The Israelites' tabernacle
   c. Solomon's palace
   d. The upper room

6. In what book of the Bible do we read, "Your lips are like a scarlet ribbon; your mouth is lovely"?
   a. Genesis
   b. Ecclesiastes
   c. Song of Songs
   d. 1 Corinthians

7. Who tied a scarlet cord in her window to be spared by the invading Israelite army?
   a. Deborah
   b. Ruth
   c. Michal
   d. Rahab

8. Finish this sentence: "Come now, let us reason together, says the Lord. Though your sins are like scarlet, they shall be ____" (Isa. 1:18).
   a. as white as snow
   b. as clear as running water
   c. removed as far as the east is from the west
   d. covered by the blood

9. In Proverbs 31:21, a woman is described in this way: "When it snows, she has no fear for her household; for all of them are clothed in scarlet." Who is she?
   a. Bathsheba
   b. Dorcas
   c. "A wife of noble character"
   d. "The daughter of Zion"

10. What biblical sufferer said, "My face is red with weeping, deep shadows ring my eyes; yet my hands have been free of violence and my prayer is pure"?
    a. Adam
    b. David
    c. Job
    d. Jesus

MULTIPLE CHOICE

7

Big and Little

1. Once a boy offered Jesus two small fish. What else did he give Jesus (John 6:9)?
   a. Tartar sauce
   b. A silver coin
   c. Five small barley loaves
   d. Seven ears of corn

2. What early king of Israel was "a head taller" than any of the other Israelites?
   a. Samuel
   b. Saul
   c. David
   d. Goliath

3. Zacchaeus was too short to see over the crowd when Jesus came to town. So what did he do?
   a. Climbed a tree
   b. Went home and moped
   c. Paid Judas to betray Jesus
   d. Rented the upper room

4. On what sea did the disciples catch 153 large fish after Jesus' resurrection?
   a. The Mediterranean Sea (or Great Sea)
   b. The Red Sea (or Sea of Reeds)
   c. The Sea of Galilee (or Sea of Tiberias)
   d. The Dead Sea

5. Who said, "Until heaven and earth disappear, not the smallest letter, not the least stroke of a pen, will by any means disappear from the Law until everything is accomplished"?
   a. Moses, on Mount Sinai
   b. Isaiah, in his Servant Song
   c. Jesus, in the Sermon on the Mount
   d. John, at the end of the book of Revelation

6. What rebellious prince died after getting his long hair caught in a large oak tree?
   a. Hophni
   b. Jonathan
   c. Absalom
   d. Amnon

7. Whose mother made him a little robe each year, which she took to the Lord's house?
   a. Moses' mother Jochebed
   b. Samuel's mother Hannah
   c. Obed's mother Ruth
   d. Jesus' mother Mary

8. Who stood over nine feet tall and wore armor weighing 125 pounds?
   a. Methuselah
   b. Saul
   c. Goliath
   d. Assyrian king Pul

9. James says that large ships are steered by small rudders. What small body part has a similar effect in our life?
   a. The tongue
   b. The heart
   c. The eye
   d. The toe

10. Who was swallowed by a "great fish"?
    a. David
    b. Daniel
    c. Peter
    d. Jonah

MULTIPLE CHOICE

8

Grounds for Action

1. Who placed a lamb's fleece on the ground in order to find out God's will?
   a. Moses
   b. Noah
   c. Samson
   d. Gideon

2. What became a snake when Moses threw it on the ground?
   a. The tablet of stone
   b. His staff
   c. The golden calf
   d. The fleece

3. Jesus said, "Not one of them will fall to the ground apart from the will of your Father" (Matt. 10:29). One of *what?* What was Jesus talking about?
   a. Clouds
   b. Birds
   c. Trees
   d. Disciples

4. What did the Israelites walk through "on dry ground"?
   a. The Red Sea
   b. The Jordan River
   c. The Sinai Desert
   d. The Sea of Galilee

5. Who fell to the ground on the road to Damascus?
   a. Saul, also known as Paul
   b. Simon, also known as Peter
   c. Joseph, also known as Barnabas
   d. Pontius Pilate

6. Who fell to the ground after Jesus said, "I am he"?
   a. Jesus' sleepy disciples
   b. The crowd in Jesus' hometown
   c. The Greeks who were asking about Jesus' identity
   d. The soldiers who came to arrest Jesus

7. Eutychus (YOU-ti-kuss) fell to the ground while Paul was preaching (Acts 20:9). Where was he sitting?
   a. In a tree
   b. In a third-story window
   c. In the back row
   d. On the back of his chariot

8. Who looked out on his 601st birthday and "saw that the surface of the ground was dry"?
   a. Methuselah
   b. Noah
   c. Abraham
   d. Elijah

9. Who "fell facedown on the ground" after a stone hit him in the forehead?
   a. Goliath
   b. Ahab
   c. Absalom
   d. Stephen

10. Jesus' disciples fell facedown on the ground when they saw Jesus in a bright cloud with which two Old Testament people?
    a. Adam and Eve
    b. Moses and Aaron
    c. Moses and Elijah
    d. Abraham and David

MULTIPLE CHOICE

9

Kings and Queens

1. Who was the king of Salem to whom Abraham gave a tenth of everything he owned?
   a. Lot
   b. Pharaoh
   c. Abimelech
   d. Melchizedek

2. Who was the wicked queen who wanted to kill Elijah?
   a. Salome
   b. Jezebel
   c. Esther
   d. Lydia

3. What king had 15 years added to his life after he prayed?
   a. David
   b. Solomon
   c. Hezekiah
   d. Joash

4. What king heard Paul's testimony and said, "Do you think that in such a short time you can persuade me to be a Christian?"
   a. Pontius Pilate
   b. Tiberius Caesar
   c. Herod Agrippa
   d. Antiochus Epiphanes

5. The queen of Sheba traveled far to see the wealth and wisdom of what king?
   a. Solomon
   b. Croesus
   c. Pharaoh
   d. Nebuchadnezzar

6. One king had a dream and asked his advisors to tell him not only what it meant, but what it *was*. Only Daniel could do this. Who was this king?
   a. Pharaoh
   b. Nebuchadnezzar

c. Belshazzar
d. Darius

7. Another king dreamed of seven fat cows and seven lean cows, and Joseph had to interpret. What did this dream mean?
   a. The rich would get richer, the poor poorer.
   b. The king needed to divide the country's livestock and kill the weaker half.
   c. The kingdom would be conquered by an allied force of seven nations.
   d. There would be seven years of plenty, followed by seven years of famine.

8. Who won a beauty contest and became queen of Persia?
   a. Bathsheba
   b. Vashti
   c. Ruth
   d. Esther

9. What wicked queen had the whole royal family killed, except for young Joash, who was hidden?
   a. Jezebel
   b. Athaliah
   c. Bernice
   d. Salome

10. What king made preparations for the building of the temple but was not allowed to build it?
    a. Saul
    b. David
    c. Solomon
    d. Jeroboam

MULTIPLE CHOICE

10

Hear! Hear!

1. If you hear the Word and obey it, Jesus said, you're like a man who builds his house on a rock. Who are you like if you hear the Word and don't obey it?
   a. A bratty child
   b. A man who builds his house on the sand
   c. A man who builds his house under a rock
   d. A man who hides treasure in a field

2. Who got his ear cut off by Peter and replaced by Jesus?
   a. A servant named Malchus
   b. A soldier named Marcus
   c. A Pharisee named Malachi
   d. A disciple named John Mark

3. Who laughed when she heard the news that she would have a baby?
   a. Mary
   b. Elizabeth
   c. Sarah
   d. Ruth

4. Who overheard plans to ambush Paul and kill him?
   a. Mary's son Mark
   b. John's brother James
   c. Rhoda's sister
   d. Paul's nephew

5. A boy heard God calling him but thought it was the priest he lived with. Who was the boy?
   a. Isaac
   b. Samuel
   c. David
   d. Jonathan

6. Whose blood did God hear "crying out" from the ground?
   a. Abel's
   b. Uriah's
   c. Saul's
   d. Jesus'

7. Who heard that there was grain in Egypt and sent his sons to get some?
   a. Noah
   b. Jacob
   c. Boaz
   d. Elisha

8. To whom did God say, "I have indeed seen the misery of my people in Egypt. I have heard them crying out because of their slave drivers, and I am concerned about their suffering"?
   a. Joseph
   b. Pharaoh
   c. Moses
   d. Joshua

9. Who wept when he heard that the wall of Jerusalem was broken down?
   a. Joshua
   b. Solomon
   c. Nehemiah
   d. Daniel

10. Who heard about the fame of Solomon and came to test him with hard questions?
    a. The queen of Sheba
    b. Hiram of Tyre
    c. "The Preacher" of Ecclesiastes
    d. Jeroboam

CATEGORIES

Pyramid

We can draw some new ideas from the TV game show " The Million-Dollar Pyramid" (or whatever amount they're giving away nowadays). That show deals with *categories*. My favorite part of the show is the end, where one person names items and the other has to guess what category they all fit into.

We're going to try some variations on that theme. In the questions below, a series of names or items is given. In each list, all have something in common. Maybe it's what they did or people they were associated with or even how their names are spelled. See if you can guess what they have in common.

Playing notes: Sometimes extra clues are given in parentheses. If you're the quizmaster, ask for guesses before you give these extra clues. Then, if no one gets it, give the items in parentheses.

As an extra game, if you guess right, see if you can add anyone or anything else to the category.

1. Peter   Andrew
   James   John
   Jonah
   (Jesus' tax payment)

2. Jonah   Mark
   Jude   Ruth
   (but not Paul or Acts)

3. Baal   Agrippa
   Matthew   Aaron
   Hannah

4. Naaman   Miriam
   Hezekiah
   (Peter's mother-in-law)

5. Abraham   Joseph
   Joseph's brothers
   Joseph and Mary

6. Rahab   Caleb
   Joab   Horeb

7. Abraham   Noah
   Elijah (on Mt. Carmel)
   Moses
   (the Israelites after crossing the Jordan)

8. The queen of Sheba
   Martha's sister Mary
   the magi
   the boy with the loaves and fish

9. Nathan   Esther
   the magi   Paul
   David as a musician
   (Abraham before Melchizedek)

10. Amos   David
    Zipporah (Moses' wife)
    a leader prophesied by Zechariah
    (people who saw baby Jesus)

15

CATEGORIES

Do-It-Yourself Pyramid

Now try the same thing, only you come up with the lists. You need at least two people for this. One of you looks at the category listed and tries to say anything that fits in that category. The others have to guess what the category is.

Playing note: Some of these are pretty hard, so feel free to skip over anything you can't deal with.

1. Old Testament books

2. Children of Jacob

3. Names that end in a vowel

4. Bible characters who got angry

5. Parables of Jesus

6. Things that Moses might say

7. Churches Paul wrote to

8. People who talked with Jesus

9. Enemies of the Israelites

10. Things that David might say

Do-It-Yourself Pyramid (cont.)

11. Prophets

_____   _____
_____   _____
_____   _____
_____   _____

17. Verses from Romans

_____   _____
_____   _____
_____   _____
_____   _____

12. Meals in the Bible

_____   _____
_____   _____
_____   _____
_____   _____

18. Verses from John

_____   _____
_____   _____
_____   _____
_____   _____

13. Names with one syllable

_____   _____
_____   _____
_____   _____
_____   _____

19. Things that Peter might say

_____   _____
_____   _____
_____   _____
_____   _____

14. Judges of Israel

_____   _____
_____   _____
_____   _____
_____   _____

20. Birds mentioned in the Bible

_____   _____
_____   _____
_____   _____
_____   _____

15. Mothers

_____   _____
_____   _____
_____   _____
_____   _____

21. Father-son combinations

_____   _____
_____   _____
_____   _____
_____   _____

16. People who slept

_____   _____
_____   _____
_____   _____
_____   _____

22. Young people

_____   _____
_____   _____
_____   _____
_____   _____

CATEGORIES

Do-It-Yourself Pyramid (cont.)

23. Things that Paul might tell Timothy

27. Disciples of Jesus

24. Names that start with *A*

28. The Ten Commandments

25. People who ran away

29. People who sang

26. Quotations from the Psalms

30. Things the shepherds might say after seeing the angels

CATEGORIES

3

"Feud"

There's another TV show that names a category and asks people to guess what the studio audience said. You get points according to how many people answered that way. Well, we don't have a studio audience, but I have asked a number of friends to list their answers, and the results are in the back of this book. So go to it! There are many possible answers. You're trying to guess what most people said.

Playing hints: This goes a lot better with one person acting as quizmaster. That person should turn to the Answers section at the back of the book. If you're familiar with the TV show *Family Feud* format, you can play it that way. Or have individuals take turns giving answers and gaining points for each right one. Or just have the whole group try to guess before getting three strikes.

If you're playing this by yourself, here's how. Pick the questions you want to play. Then write down your answers in order. Take the number of "answers available" and add three. That's the number of answers you should write down. For example, if there are six available answers, you would add three to get nine answers you are to write down. Then, check the Answers section, and total up your points as you go down your list. But as soon as you have gotten three wrong—stop. Even if you have correct answers farther down the list, they don't count. You have struck out.

Remember: You are not just trying to guess right answers. You are trying to guess the answers that most people would say.

Also, a person's answer does not have to match word for word with the answer we give. If they get the idea, that's close enough.

"Feud" Questions

1. List a miracle Jesus did.
   (5 available answers)

2. Name an author of a book of the Bible.
   (6 available answers)

3. Name a Bible character who lied.
   (6 available answers)

4. Name a city or town mentioned in the Bible. (6 available answers)

5. Name two back-to-back books of the Bible. (5 available answers)

6. Name a king mentioned in the Bible.
   (7 available answers)

CATEGORIES

"Feud" (cont.)

7. Name an animal mentioned in the Bible. (6 available answers)

8. List a time in the Bible when people sang. (11 available answers)

9. List something that David did. (6 available answers)

10. List something that Moses did. (7 available answers)

11. Name a tribe of Israel. (4 available answers)

12. Name a town that Paul visited. (6 available answers)

STEP QUIZZES

In each of the following quizzes, there are five clues for the same answer. These clues are graded according to difficulty, with the hardest (level 5) coming first. This allows several variations in quiz giving.

Age level/handicap: Each player is assigned a level according to his or her age or ability. Young children would be at level 1, while the keenest Bible scholars would be at level 5. The play passes around the group, with each player receiving the clue at his or her level. (Players may ask for all previous, or higher-numbered, clues.)

Bidding: If all players have about the same Bible knowledge, try bidding for questions. Start the bidding at level 1, of course, and go up to level 5. The player who wins the bid will receive all the clues down to that level. That is, if a player bids level 4, he receives the level 5 clue and the level 4 clue, but no more. If he gets it right, he gets the number of points he bid. If he misses, he loses that amount.

Point play: The play passes around the group, with each player having a turn at a question. The clues are given, beginning with level 5. If the player guesses correctly at level 5, she gets five points. If not, she gets the level 4 clue. If she guesses then, she gets four points. If not, she gets the next clue, and so on.

(This can also be done with call-outs, instead of taking turns, but this will only work if all players are about the same level. Give each clue and invite anyone to call out the answer. Whoever guesses right gets the number of points corresponding to the level of the clue just given.)

Chance: Players take turns, but each player rolls a die to determine his level. Roll a six, and you lose a turn. With any other number, you receive all the clues down to that number. (If you're on the road and you don't have dice, look for the first number [one through five] on the next license plate or sign that you see.)

Notes: In some cases, a particular clue will have another valid answer besides the one we're looking for. If an alternate correct answer is given, give credit for a right answer.

In some cases, you may need to ask for more information. If you're looking for "the temple" and you get "Jerusalem," it's not wrong—just ask the player to be more specific.

STEP QUIZZES

1

People

A. 5. Her name means "the life-giving one."
4. She was named by her husband.
3. A serpent told her she was lying.
2. She raised Cain.
1. She was deceived by Satan in the Garden of Eden.

B. 5. He told Pharaoh, "I have lived 130 long, hard years."
4. Abraham's sneaky grandson
3. Dad to a dozen
2. His name was changed to Israel.
1. Joseph was his favorite son.

C. 5. His book comes after the shortest one in the Old Testament.
4. He said, "The waters closed above me; the seaweed wrapped itself around my head."
3. The first day he preached in the big city, the people repented.
2. A fish spit him up onto the beach.
1. He prayed to God from inside a fish.

D. 5. Her Hebrew name was Hadassah.
4. She replaced Vashti.
3. She told the king, "This wicked Haman is our enemy."
2. Her cousin was Mordecai.
1. This queen saved her people by going to see the king without being called for.

E. 5. Og and Sihon were among the kings he defeated.
4. He was the son of Nun.
3. He prayed, "Let the sun stand still over Gibeon," and it did!
2. He went up Mount Sinai with Moses.
1. He fought the battle of Jericho.

F. 5. A seminary president, sort of
4. When he prayed, God made a whole army blind.

3. He was bald.
2. The Syrian commander Naaman went to this prophet to be healed of leprosy.
1. He parted the Jordan with Elijah's cloak.

G. 5. All his relatives assumed he would be named Zechariah.
4. Son of Zechariah and Elizabeth.
3. "I am not the Christ," he said.
2. Beheaded at Herod's command
1. He baptized Jesus.

H. 5. Methuselah was his grandfather.
4. Father of Shem, Ham, and Japheth
3. The raven he sent out did not return, but the dove did.
2. God told him to put all kinds of animals in a boat.
1. He built a 450-foot-long ark.

I. 5. Grandfather of Dan and Gad
4. He married Laban's sister.
3. Half-blind, he blessed the younger son.
2. An angel spared this child's life by holding back his father's knife.
1. Though Abraham had other children, the promises apply to this one.

J. 5. He assured the crowd that he and his friends were sober, saying: "People don't get drunk by 9:00 A.M.!"
4. He spoke with a Galilean accent.
3. He led the apostles in saying, "We must obey God rather than men."
2. Jesus once said to him, "Get away from me, you Satan!"
1. This disciple affirmed that Jesus was "the Christ, the Messiah, the Son of the living God."

STEP QUIZZES

2

People

A. 5. The only Gospel writer to include the visit of the wise men
   4. The Pharisees were upset when Jesus had dinner with swindlers in this disciple's home.
   3. He was sitting at a tax tollbooth when Jesus called him.
   2. The apostle who was a tax collector
   1. He wrote the first book of the New Testament.

B. 5. He was a farmer, son of a "gardener."
   4. The Lord gave him a permanent ID.
   3. The Lord accepted his brother's offering but not his.
   2. The first murderer
   1. He murdered his brother Abel.

C. 5. He killed a lion, and a swarm of bees made honey in its carcass.
   4. He riddled the Philistines with problems.
   3. The Philistines called him out to entertain them, and he brought down the house.
   2. He tied torches to the tails of 300 foxes and sent them running through the Philistines' fields.
   1. His strength was in his hair.

D. 5. Jacob watered the flocks of this shepherdess.
   4. Laban couldn't find the household idols she stole, because she was sitting on them.
   3. She died in childbirth on the way to Bethlehem.
   2. Mother of Joseph and Benjamin
   1. Jacob agreed—twice—to work seven years to win her as his wife.

E. 5. His father-in-law was named Jethro.
   4. He married Zipporah, a shepherd girl from Midian.
   3. When his arms grew tired, Aaron and Hur held them up while the army fought.
   2. He went up Mount Sinai and disappeared for 40 days.
   1. He said to Pharaoh, "Let my people go."

F. 5. He was nicknamed "The Twin."
   4. Jesus told him, "I am the way and the truth and the life."
   3. He was absent when Jesus first appeared to his disciples after the Resurrection.
   2. He said, "I won't believe it unless I see the nail wounds in his hands."
   1. The doubting disciple

G. 5. They asked the man born blind, "This man who opened your eyes—who do you say he is?"
   4. Gnat-straining camel-swallowers
   3. Paul was once a member of this group.
   2. Blind guides
   1. A member of this religious group asked Jesus to name the most important commandment in the law.

H. 5. He pretended to be insane so a Philistine king would spare him.
   4. He was told, "All Israel has joined Absalom in a conspiracy against you!"
   3. He once made alterations to Saul's robe.
   2. Jesse's youngest son
   1. He killed Goliath.

People (cont.)

I. 5. Because he did what the demons said, a herd of pigs rushed over a cliff and drowned.
    4. He said, "Oh, you stubborn, faithless people! How long shall I bear with you?"
    3. Soldiers threw dice to divide up his clothes.
    2. The voice said, "This is my beloved Son." Who was it talking about?
    1. He was born to a virgin.

J. 5. His father disappeared, for God just "took him away."
    4. Noah's grandfather
    3. He was 187 when his son Lamech was born—and he still outlived him.
    2. He died at age 969.
    1. The oldest man in the Bible

STEP QUIZZES

3

People

A. 5. Michal was his daughter.
   4. He consulted a medium at Endor.
   3. David once cut off the bottom of this man's robe.
   2. When he was chosen king of Israel, they found him hiding in the baggage.
   1. First king of Israel

B. 5. She said, "By now the smell will be terrible, for he has been dead four days."
   4. She was "the jittery type," worried about fixing a big dinner.
   3. She said, "Sir, if you had been here, my brother wouldn't have died."
   2. She complained that she did all the work while her sister just sat and listened to Jesus.
   1. She lived in Bethany with her brother Lazarus and her sister Mary.

C. 5. His building projects included a palace, Fort Millo, a city wall, and three cities in Israel.
   4. The foundation of the temple was laid during the fourth year of his reign.
   3. The Lord appeared to him in a dream and offered anything he wanted.
   2. In a child-custody dispute, he suggested cutting the child in two.
   1. Succeeded his father David as king of Israel

D. 5. Son of Terah
   4. He had two sons, but his brother had a Lot.
   3. His wife laughed at the prospect of having a son in their old age.
   2. God told him his descendants would be like the stars—"too many to count."
   1. At the last moment, an angel prevented him from sacrificing his son.

E. 5. Ananias helped him regain his sight.
   4. To escape his enemies, he was let down the city wall of Damascus in a basket.
   3. He heard a voice say, "I am Jesus, the one you are persecuting!"
   2. He dreamed of a man from Macedonia calling, "Come over here and help us!"
   1. Apostle to the Gentiles

F. 5. Sons of Thunder
   4. Their mother asked Jesus to let them sit on thrones next to his throne in the kingdom.
   3. The sons of Zebedee
   2. These two fishermen were in a boat with their father, mending their nets, when Jesus called them.
   1. These two, along with Peter, fell asleep in the Gethsemane garden grove while Jesus prayed.

G. 5. She nagged her boyfriend until she learned he was a Nazirite.
   4. She begged, "Please tell me . . . why you are so strong."
   3. She wove her boyfriend's hair into a loom, but when he got up, he broke the loom.
   2. Samson lied to her three times.
   1. Samson's dangerous girlfriend

H. 5. He was nicknamed Jerubbaal, meaning, "Let Baal take care of himself."
   4. Abimelech was his son.
   3. Years before Saul, this man had a chance to be Israel's king.
   2. He selected 300 men for his army by the way they drank water.
   1. He defeated the Midianites with trumpets, jars, torches, and only 300 men.

People (cont.)

I. 5. David's great-grandmother
    4. Orpah's sister-in-law
    3. She traveled with her husband's mother from Moab to Bethlehem.
    2. She married Boaz.
    1. Her mother-in-law was Naomi.

J. 5. Psalm 133 pictures oil running down his head, onto his beard and robe.
    4. When he threw down his rod before Pharaoh, it became a serpent.
    3. He and his sister criticized Moses for marrying a foreigner.
    2. Israel's first high priest
    1. Moses' brother

People

A. 5. He lived in Uz.
   4. He said, "I came naked from my mother's womb, and I shall have nothing when I die."
   3. He had 7 sons and 3 daughters, lost them, then got 10 new kids.
   2. He sat among the ashes, scraping his boils with a broken piece of pottery.
   1. Eliphaz, Bildad, and Zophar joined this sufferer on the ash heap and tried to console him.

B. 5. His first name was Joseph, but he was nicknamed "Son of Encouragement."
   4. The people of Lystra thought he was the god Jupiter.
   3. He went to Tarsus to hunt for Paul.
   2. He accompanied Paul on his first missionary journey.
   1. He split up with Paul in a squabble concerning John Mark.

C. 5. He was eager to destroy every Christian.
   4. He and his teammate were accused of turning "the world upside down."
   3. He was the coat-check guy at Stephen's stoning.
   2. On Malta, a poisonous snake bit him, but he just shook it off.
   1. This apostle met Jesus in a vision on the road to Damascus.

D. 5. Matthias was chosen to take his place.
   4. He threw money on the floor of the temple.
   3. He said Mary's perfume should have been sold and the money given to the poor.
   2. The chief priests paid him 30 silver coins.

E. 1. He asked the chief priests, "How much will you pay me to get Jesus into your hands?"

E. 5. Paul challenged this man: "Work hard so God can say to you, 'Well done.'"
   4. Eunice's son
   3. The believers in Lystra and Iconium thought well of this young man.
   2. Paul sent him to Corinth to help the Corinthians follow Paul's example.
   1. Paul wrote two epistles to him.

F. 5. He taunted, "Am I a dog, that you come at me with a stick?"
   4. Saul offered a tax exemption and marriage to his own daughter to anyone who could kill this man.
   3. A Philistine champion from Gath
   2. He was over nine feet tall.
   1. David felled him with a stone from his sling.

G. 5. In this man's time, according to Jesus, there were banquets, parties, and weddings.
   4. God told him, "I have decided to destroy all mankind."
   3. He was once the only righteous man on earth.
   2. His family was the first to see a rainbow.
   1. He was 600 years old when the Flood came.

H. 5. Well, well, well. His men dug three—the Well of Argument, the Well of Anger, and the Well of Room Enough for Us at Last.
   4. Father of "Red Stuff" and "Grabber"
   3. His wife told him, "I'm sick and tired of these local girls. I'd rather die than see Jacob marry one of them."

STEP QUIZZES

4

People (cont.)

2. His name means "Laughter," because his mother couldn't believe it.
1. Sarah's Son

I. 5. Shimei threw stones at this king and cursed him.
   4. He clubbed to death both lions and bears.
   3. He cried, "O my son Absalom, my son, my son Absalom!"
   2. He "danced before the Lord with all his might."
   1. Bathsheba's second husband

J. 5. He said, "What I have written, I have written."
   4. He had a custom of releasing one Jewish prisoner each Passover.
   3. The Jewish leaders told him, "If you release this man, you are no friend of Caesar's!"
   2. He released Barabbas.
   1. The Roman governor of Judea who tried Jesus

People

A. 5. He told a young prophet to anoint Jehu king of Israel—and then run for his life.
   4. King Joash visited this prophet on his deathbed.
   3. He told Naaman the leper to wash seven times in the Jordan River.
   2. He asked Elijah, "Please grant me twice as much prophetic power as you have had."
   1. The young prophets of Jericho proclaimed that Elijah's spirit rested on this man.

B. 5. Father of Rehoboam
   4. Jesus said that the lilies of the field are dressed better than this man.
   3. He was told by a foreign queen, "Your wisdom and prosperity are far greater than anything I've ever heard of!"
   2. He wrote, "How does a man become wise? The first step is to trust and reverence the Lord!"
   1. God told him, "I will give you a wiser mind than anyone else has ever had or ever will have!"

C. 5. His father was dumbstruck.
   4. Herod arrested him for opposing his marriage.
   3. The dancing daughter of Herodias asked for this man's head on a tray.
   2. Isaiah had prophesied about this man's ministry: "I hear a shout in the wilderness, 'Prepare a road for the Lord.'"
   1. He wore camel's hair clothing and a leather belt.

D. 5. Son of Manoah, of the tribe of Dan
   4. He sang, "Heaps upon heaps, All with a donkey's jaw!"
   3. Captors from Judah tied him with ropes, but he snapped them like thread.
   2. He was blinded by the Philistines and forced to grind grain in prison while his hair grew back.
   1. Delilah's boyfriend

E. 5. He sent his servant to Iraq to find a wife for his son.
   4. Melchizedek blessed him.
   3. He pleaded with God to save Sodom.
   2. He was 100 years old when Isaac was born.
   1. Isaac's father

F. 5. These people said that Jesus could cast out demons because he himself was Satan.
   4. Jesus likened them to beautiful mausoleums (tombs).
   3. Jesus told a story of one of these people and a tax collector going to the temple to pray.
   2. At the Triumphal Entry, these people asked Jesus to quiet the crowd.
   1. Jesus told this religious group, "I, the Messiah, am master even of the Sabbath."

G. 5. He killed Zebah and Zalmunna, kings of Midian.
   4. He vandalized the altar of Baal by hitching an ox to it and pulling it down.
   3. The Ephraimites were offended by being excluded from his band of 300.

People (cont.)

2. He tested the Lord's calling by placing a fleece on the ground.
1. His army won by blowing trumpets and breaking jars.

H. 5. Dinah was his daughter.
4. His name means "Cheater" or "Grabber."
3. His twin brother might have complained, "Mother always loved you best."
2. He traded a bowl of stew for the rights of the first son.
1. Esau's twin

I. 5. God made a vine grow quickly to shelter this man from the sun.
4. The ship to Tarshish was in a terrible storm until the sailors threw this man overboard.
3. When God changed his mind and showed mercy to the city, this prophet got angry.
2. Due to this man's preaching, the people of Nineveh wore sackcloth.
1. He was inside a fish three days and nights.

J. 5. Elihu was a fourth friend of this man.
4. God told this man, "Take a look at the hippopotamus. I made him, too."
3. The Lord told Satan how righteous this man was.
2. His wife advised him to curse God and die.
1. The Lord allowed Satan to afflict this good man.

STEP QUIZZES

People

A. 5. He said, "Good salt is worthless if it loses its saltiness."
   4. "Why are you crying?" he asked Mary.
   3. When he was a baby, Simeon and Anna met him at the temple.
   2. He fed 4,000 men, besides the women and children, with seven loaves and a few fish.
   1. He was born in Bethlehem during Herod's reign.

B. 5. He wrote letters to a man named Gaius and to "the chosen lady" (or "that dear woman").
   4. He wrote down Jesus' messages for seven churches in Turkey.
   3. He outran Peter to Jesus' tomb.
   2. On the cross, Jesus put his mother in the care of this disciple.
   1. Disciple who was Jesus' closest friend

C. 5. He was the most handsome man in Israel, head and shoulders taller than anyone else.
   4. When his armor-bearer refused to kill him, he fell on his own sword and died.
   3. He went to Samuel for help in finding stray donkeys.
   2. This king threw a spear at his court musician.
   1. The father of David's friend Jonathan

D. 5. He said, "Master, to whom shall we go? You alone have the words that give eternal life."
   4. Jesus asked this man, "Do you love me more than these others?"
   3. He assured Jesus that he would never desert him.
   2. Andrew's brother
   1. Jesus said to him, "Upon this rock I will build my church."

E. 5. Isaiah urged the Jews not to trust in this leader for protection.
   4. This leader's sorcerers were unable to duplicate the miracles of Aaron's rod.
   3. This man had a dream about seven fat cows and seven skinny cows.
   2. This leader's cavalry drowned.
   1. Moses gave this man God's message: "Let my people go!"

F. 5. Paul asked this man to bring a cloak and some books and parchments when he came to visit.
   4. Paul warned him, "The love of money is the first step toward all kinds of sin."
   3. Paul urged this man to be a good soldier of Christ Jesus.
   2. Paul reminded this Christian, "When you were a small child, you were taught the Holy Scriptures."
   1. This young man was with Paul when the apostle wrote 2 Corinthians, Philippians, and three other letters.

G. 5. This was the most famous child of Amram and Jochebed.
   4. His mother was paid to be his nurse.
   3. His name means "to draw out," since he was drawn from the water.
   2. The Angel of Jehovah appeared to this man in a burning bush.
   1. Aaron's brother

H. 5. His father named him by writing the name on paper.
   4. Jesus said that in all humanity there was none greater than this man.
   3. As Jesus did later, this preacher called the religious leaders "sons of snakes."

2. He ate locusts and wild honey.
1. He baptized with water and waited for the one who would baptize with the Holy Spirit.

I. 5. This man said, "If I were tied with seven raw-leather bowstrings, I would become as weak as anyone else."
4. He said to the boy who was leading him, "Place my hands against the two pillars."
3. He canceled his wedding when the bride gave the Philistines the answer to his riddle.

2. This man killed 1,000 Philistines with a donkey's jawbone.
1. He lied three times to Delilah about what gave him his strength.

J. 5. Brother of Nahor and Haran
4. He believed God, and that is why God canceled his sins and declared him "not guilty."
3. Father of Ishmael
2. God told him to sacrifice Isaac.
1. Husband of Sarah

7

People

A. 5. After Christ's ascension, this disciple suggested choosing someone to take Judas's place.
   4. Jesus told this man to catch a fish and pay his tax with the coin found in its mouth.
   3. This disciple took Jesus aside and assured him that he would not be killed.
   2. He said to Jesus, "Wash my hands and head as well—not just my feet!"
   1. The disciple who walked on water toward Jesus

B. 5. God called this man "son of dust."
   4. This man lay on his left side for 390 days to symbolize Israel's 390 years of captivity and doom.
   3. God had this prophet shave his head and beard with a sword and divide the hair into three parts.
   2. This prophet saw a vision of "whirl-wheels."
   1. This prophet was carried by the Spirit to a valley full of old, dry bones.

C. 5. He served bread and fish at a post-resurrection breakfast.
   4. A "priest forever, with the same rank as Melchizedek."
   3. Though he was God, he did not demand and cling to his rights as God.
   2. The Morning Star
   1. Astrologers (wise men) brought this baby gold, frankincense, and myrrh.

D. 5. This king's home was Gibeah.
   4. He sinned by making a sacrifice before a battle.
   3. Samuel went gaga when this king did not kill Agag.
   2. Before David killed Goliath, he tried on this man's armor.
   1. David's predecessor and predator

E. 5. Instead of going east, he boarded a ship for Tarshish.
   4. Jesus referred to this prophet in predicting his own resurrection.
   3. A fish's indigestion
   2. The Lord sent him to Nineveh with a message of doom.
   1. A great fish swallowed this disobedient prophet.

F. 5. He said, "I will not let you go until you bless me!"
   4. Reuben was his oldest son.
   3. Leah's husband
   2. He worked 14 years in all to marry his sweetheart.
   1. He was in love with Rachel.

G. 5. He pretended his wife was his sister—twice.
   4. At age 75, he was told to leave his country.
   3. Choosing land, he gave Lot the best lots.
   2. Isaac and Ishmael buried him in the cave of Mach-pelah.
   1. Father of a multitude of nations

H. 5. This man preached, "If you have two coats, give one to the poor."
   4. His disciples asked why Jesus' disciples did not fast.
   3. Jesus called him Elijah.
   2. He said, "Look! There is the Lamb of God who takes away the world's sin."
   1. He didn't want to baptize Jesus.

7

People (cont.)

I. 5. He commanded his morticians to embalm Jacob's body.

4. Eleventh son of Jacob

3. Reuben argued against killing him.

2. After this man interpreted Pharaoh's dream, Pharaoh made him second in command.

1. Slave of Potiphar and vice-Pharaoh of Egypt were two positions he had.

J. 5. His money was used to buy a field used by potters and to make it a cemetery.

4. Jesus told this man, "My friend, go ahead and do what you have come for."

3. He was in charge of the disciples' funds.

2. He arrived in Gethsemane with a mob armed with swords and clubs.

1. He betrayed Jesus with a kiss.

STEP QUIZZES

8

People

A. 5. The only Gospel writer to tell about angels appearing to the shepherds in Bethlehem
   4. He wrote two books to Theophilus, whose name means, "Friend who loves God."
   3. The "dear doctor" who traveled with Paul
   2. He wrote the Acts of the Apostles.
   1. Author of the third Gospel

B. 5. He wrestled with a man who put his hip out of joint.
   4. He increased his flocks by tricking Laban.
   3. At Bethel he dreamed of a stairway to heaven.
   2. He put on Esau's clothes to trick his father.
   1. He was father of the 12 sons who became the patriarchs of the tribes of Israel.

C. 5. This man preached, "There is salvation in no one else! Under all heaven there is no other name for men to call upon to save them."
   4. He asked, "How often should I forgive a brother who sins against me? Seven times?"
   3. He went inside Christ's tomb and saw the grave clothes.
   2. After the Resurrection, this disciple announced, "I'm going fishing."
   1. Despite this man's objections, Jesus washed his feet.

D. 5. He was opposed by Sanballat and Tobiah.
   4. For his 12 years as governor of Judah, he accepted no salary.
   3. Because of their enemies, this leader arranged that half the builders worked on the wall while the others stood guard.
   2. He asked the Persian king, "Send me to Judah to rebuild the city of my fathers!"
   1. Cupbearer for the king of Persia before he returned to Jerusalem to rebuild the walls

E. 5. The Lord had him name his son Maher-shalal-hash-baz.
   4. An angel touched this man's lips with a burning coal.
   3. He wrote of a "man of sorrows" who was wounded for our sins.
   2. He wrote, "For unto us a child is born; unto us a son is given."
   1. This prophet saw the Lord on his throne, with six-winged angels singing, "Holy, holy, holy."

F. 5. Follows Boaz and Obed in Jesus' genealogy
   4. Father of Eliab, Abinadab, and Shammah, among others
   3. This man of Bethlehem had eight sons in all.
   2. Saul wrote to this man, "Please let David join my staff, for I am very fond of him."
   1. David's father

People (cont.)

G.
5. God told Abraham that this son would become a great nation with 12 princes among his descendants.
4. He helped Isaac bury Abraham.
3. He teased young Isaac.
2. His name means "God hears," because God heard Hagar's woes.
1. Son of Abraham and Hagar

H.
5. She died at Kadesh in the wilderness of Zin.
4. She was struck with leprosy and confined outside the Israeli camp for seven days.
3. She and her brother criticized Moses about his wife.
2. Playing a timbrel, she led Israeli women in dances.
1. Aaron's sister

I.
5. "Are you the Jews' Messiah?" he asked Jesus.
4. Jesus told him, "My kingdom is not of the world."
3. His wife had a nightmare about Jesus.
2. He posted a sign on the cross calling Jesus the King of the Jews.
1. This Roman ruler washed his hands of the blood of Jesus.

J.
5. The chief priests plotted to kill this man since many were believing in Jesus because of him.
4. Jesus told his disciples that this man had "gone to sleep."
3. He had been dead for four days by the time Jesus arrived.
2. Jesus yelled into the tomb for this man to come out.
1. Brother of Mary and Martha

People

A. 5. He predicted a time when people will beg the mountains to fall and crush them.
4. He invited himself to dinner with a tax collector.
3. Faced with a difficult question, he stooped down and wrote in the dust with his finger.
2. He saved Peter from drowning.
1. John didn't want to baptize him.

B. 5. He debated with members of a Jewish cult called "The Freedmen."
4. This deacon was "unusually full of faith and the Holy Spirit."
3. His defense speech is found in Acts 7.
2. Those who stoned him laid their coats at Paul's feet.
1. He was stoned by Jewish leaders for his witness for Christ.

C. 5. The tribe of his descendants was nearly wiped out in battle with the other tribes of Israel.
4. King Saul and the apostle Paul were both descendants of this son of Jacob.
3. Joseph tried to frame him by having a silver cup placed in his sack of grain.
2. Joseph's only full brother
1. Youngest son of Jacob

D. 5. Naphtali's grandmother
4. She offered to draw water for the camels of Abraham's servant.
3. Isaac was meditating in the fields when he saw the camels coming, bringing her.
2. She told Jacob that Esau was threatening his life.
1. Jacob was her favorite son.

E. 5. "Did the prophets tell us where the Messiah would be born?" he asked the religious leaders.
4. He asked the astrologers to go to Bethlehem, find the child, and return to him.
3. He ordered his soldiers to kill every baby boy in Bethlehem two years old and under.
2. Joseph and Mary fled to Egypt until his death.
1. He was king of Judea when Jesus was born.

F. 5. This wonderful Bible teacher wowed the people of Corinth.
4. If Paul was the planter, this man was the waterer.
3. In Ephesus, he preached the message of John the Baptist.
2. Priscilla and Aquila had to explain to him that the Messiah had already come.
1. A wonderful Bible teacher from Alexandria who taught in Corinth and Ephesus

G. 5. He had Adonijah, Joab, and Shimei killed to secure his grip on the kingdom.
4. Last king of the united kingdom of Israel
3. The songbook that bears his name begins: "Kiss me again and again, for your love is sweeter than wine."
2. Wise guy
1. He had 700 wives and 300 concubines.

People (cont.)

H. 5. He was more wicked than any other king of Israel.
   4. He didn't like Micaiah's prophecies because they were always gloomy.
   3. The prophet told him, "Isn't killing Naboth bad enough? Must you rob him, too?"
   2. Elijah told him, "There won't be any dew or rain for several years until I say the word."
   1. He married Jezebel.

I. 5. A disciple of John who became a disciple of Jesus.
   4. He and Philip told Jesus about the Greeks who wanted to meet him.
   3. He introduced Jesus to a youngster with five loaves and a couple of fish.
   2. He found his brother and told him, "We have found the Messiah!"
   1. He and his brother, Simon Peter, were commercial fishermen.

J. 5. He brought 100 pounds of ointment to embalm Jesus' body.
   4. He said to Jesus, "Sir, we all know that God has sent you to teach us."
   3. This Pharisee came to Jesus after dark.
   2. This Jewish religious leader's interview with Jesus is reported in John 3.
   1. Jesus told this leader, "Unless you are born again, you can never get into the Kingdom of God."

STEP QUIZZES

10

People

A.
5. In Galatians, Paul uses this slave-wife to represent the slavery to the law.
4. An angel appeared to her as she ran away from Sarah and told her to return.
3. Sarah's maid
2. Sarah gave this Egyptian servant girl to Abraham as his wife so he could have a son.
1. Ishmael's mother

B.
5. A secret disciple of Jesus, for fear of the religious leaders
4. A member of the Supreme Court who didn't agree with what they did to Jesus
3. He and Nicodemus wrapped Jesus' body in a linen cloth.
2. He asked Pilate for Jesus' body.
1. Jesus was buried in this rich man's tomb.

C.
5. Her sister had lovely eyes, but this woman was shapely, a beauty in every way.
4. She became envious of her sister, who was bearing children.
3. Bilhah was her maid.
2. Jeremiah pictured her weeping for her children.
1. She and Leah were daughters of Laban.

D.
5. He wrote, "The Sun of Righteousness will rise with healing in his wings."
4. His book follows Zechariah's.
3. "Will a man rob God?" his book asks, accusing Israel of withholding tithes.
2. His book promised that another prophet like Elijah would come before Judgment Day.
1. He wrote the last book of the Old Testament.

E.
5. He was hired by Balak to curse the Israelites.
4. He was a prophet for profit, as Jude and Peter wrote later.
3. A donkey crushed his foot against a wall.
2. If his donkey hadn't balked, an angel would have killed him.
1. His donkey said to him, "What have I done that deserves your beating me?"

F.
5. At David's command, Hushai the Archite gave this man bad advice.
4. Joab killed him, though David had ordered that he not be harmed.
3. Riding through the forest, he was "hair today, gone tomorrow."
2. His hair got caught in a tree as he rode under it; this led to his death.
1. This prince led a rebellion against his father, David.

G.
5. He and Jacob set up a monument to make sure they kept their agreement.
4. He gave Jacob all the black sheep from his flock.
3. Joseph's other grandfather, besides Isaac
2. He tricked Jacob into seven extra years of work.
1. Father of Rachel and Leah

H.
5. The second of seven deacons chosen by the early church
4. Simon the sorcerer was converted through this man's preaching.
3. He had four unmarried daughters with the gift of prophecy.
2. He explained Scripture to the treasurer of Ethiopia.
1. The Ethiopian said to him, "Look! Water! Why can't I be baptized?"

People (cont.)

I. 5. Jesus told this man, "Put your sword away."
    4. He raised Dorcas from the dead.
    3. Though he was double-chained between two soldiers, an angel got him out of prison.
    2. Jesus healed this man's mother-in-law from a high fever.
    1. His name means "the rock."

J. 5. The night this Chaldean king was killed, Darius the Mede entered Babylon.
    4. At a feast in Babylon, this king had the cups from the Jerusalem temple brought out for toasts.
    3. He saw the handwriting on the wall.
    2. This man was so frightened by the writing on the wall that his knees knocked together.
    1. Daniel explained to this king the meaning of what God had written on the wall—his kingdom was doomed.

Places

A. 5. The "Tower of Siloam tragedy" occurred in this city.
   4. Jesus prophesied that this city would be conquered.
   3. A psalmist said that if he forgot this city, his right hand might as well forget how to play the harp.
   2. City where Jesus' parents lost him at age 12
   1. Jesus was crucified just outside of this city.

B. 5. Town where a Moabite girl found a husband
   4. Naomi and Ruth returned there at the beginning of barley harvest.
   3. In the marketplace of this city, Boaz made legal arrangements to marry Ruth.
   2. Herod had all the babies in this city killed.
   1. Where Jesus was born

C. 5. Also known as the Sea of Tiberias
   4. Where Jesus stilled a storm
   3. Where Simon Peter and Andrew were fishing when Jesus called them
   2. By this sea, Jesus fed 4,000 men (plus women and children) with seven loaves and a few fish.
   1. The water Jesus walked on

D. 5. The Arabs called it Mount Hagar.
   4. Law-giving locale
   3. Where Elijah went when he was depressed
   2. Moses saw the burning bush near this mountain.
   1. Where God gave the Ten Commandments

E. 5. Neco was king of this country.
   4. Country where Jacob died
   3. Frogs, at one time, covered this nation.
   2. Country where Sarah was a member of Pharaoh's harem
   1. Moses told the leader of this land, "Let my people go!"

F. 5. Paul told the elders of the church in this city, "Be sure that you feed and shepherd God's flock."
   4. Where a demon said to a would-be exorcist, "I know Jesus and I know Paul, but who are you?"
   3. Timothy was a pastor-teacher in this church when Paul wrote him.
   2. Demetrius the silversmith led a revolt in this city against Paul.
   1. Paul wrote to the church in this city, "Put on all of God's armor."

G. 5. The assassins of King Sennacherib escaped to an area of this mountain.
   4. The dove returned here twice but not the third time.
   3. Where eight people made a new start
   2. This peak appeared again 150 days after the rain started.
   1. Where the ark parked

H. 5. All the people in this city seemed to spend their time discussing new ideas.
   4. In this city, Paul quoted a local poet: "We are the sons of God."
   3. Stoics and Epicureans in this city thought Paul was a dreamer.
   2. Where the altar "To the Unknown God" was
   1. Where Mars Hill is

Places (cont.)

I.
5. As a baby, King Joash was hidden in a storeroom here.
4. In a vision, a man with a tape measure gave Ezekiel precise measurements for this.
3. Paul was accused of bringing Gentiles into this place.
2. Solomon employed over 180,000 workers in building this.
1. Through Jeremiah (and later Jesus), God called this a "den of robbers."

J.
5. Leaving this city, Jesus heard a voice call, "O Son of David, have mercy on me!"
4. Where a tax collector promised to give back four times as much to anyone he had overcharged
3. The Good Samaritan helped a man who was mugged on a trip between Jerusalem and this city.
2. Joshua cursed this ruined city— the oldest and youngest sons of anyone rebuilding it would die.
1. The Israelites walked around this city 13 times.

Places

A. 5. The Lord promised, through Isaiah, that he would make this superpower a desolate land of porcupines.
4. "Mene Mene Tekel Parsin" meant doom for this nation.
3. The psalmist sang about hanging harps on the willows, sitting by the rivers of this land.
2. Where Daniel was chief magistrate
1. This nation held the Jews captive for 70 years.

B. 5. The young prophets of this city declared, "The spirit of Elijah rests upon Elisha!"
4. Where two spies hid under piles of flax
3. Where Achan was takin', though the rules he was breakin'
2. Joshua sent two spies here.
1. Its walls came a-tumblin' down.

C. 5. The river that ran through this place had four branches: the Pishon, Gihon, Tigris, and Euphrates.
4. A nudist colony, of sorts
3. First scene of sin
2. The Tree of Conscience was there.
1. Home to Adam and Eve

D. 5. Where the ax head floated
4. Elisha told Naaman, the Syrian captain, to wash seven times in this river.
3. Elijah struck it with his cloak, and it parted.
2. Under Joshua's command, the Israelites walked through this on dry ground.
1. Jesus was baptized in it.

E. 5. Rufus lived here.
4. Writing to Philippi from this city, Paul sends greetings from "those who work in Caesar's palace."
3. Paul planned to stop there on his way to Spain.
2. Paul wrote to the church in this city, "The wages of sin is death, but the free gift of God is eternal life."
1. Paul was a citizen of the empire based in this city.

F. 5. Nahum prophesied the destruction of this city.
4. This city was so large that it took three days to walk around it.
3. A prophet eventually got there but only after a "fish dinner."
2. According to the book of Jonah, this city had 120,000 people.
1. When Jonah preached there, the people repented.

G. 5. On the banks of this sea, the Israelites sang, "I will sing to the Lord, for he has triumphed gloriously."
4. Where the Lord told Moses, "Quit praying and get the people moving!"
3. Miriam danced near this body of water.
2. Where Pharaoh's horsemen drowned
1. At Moses' command, the Israelites walked through this sea on dry ground.

H. 5. The people here mobbed Jesus and nearly pushed him over a cliff, but Jesus walked away through the crowd.
4. The people in this town asked, "Isn't this Joseph's son?"
3. Nathanael quipped about this town, "Can anything good come from there?"

Places (cont.)

2. Where Mary was when Gabriel announced that she would bear Jesus
1. Where Jesus grew up

I. 5. In a way, God's action at Pentecost reversed his action here.
4. Building project of a one-tongued people
3. It means "confusion."
2. Would-be site of the first skyscraper
1. Tower where God confused the languages

J. 5. Judas knew the place.
4. Where Malchus lost an ear and got it back
3. Where Judas showed up with an armed mob
2. Garden where Jesus' disciples fell asleep
1. Where Jesus prayed before his crucifixion, "My Father! If it is possible, let this cup be taken away from me."

Places

A. 5. David's men broke through battle lines to get him some water from this city, but David wouldn't drink it.
   4. Where the Lord told Samuel, "Men judge by outward appearance, but I look at a man's thoughts and intentions."
   3. Jesse and his sons lived in this town.
   2. Micah prophesied that this village would produce an everlasting king.
   1. Herod told the astrologers (wise men) to go to this city and then return to the royal court.

B. 5. Near this town, on the outskirts of Jerusalem, Jesus cursed a fig tree.
   4. A woman poured expensive perfume over Jesus' head while he stayed at Simon's house in this town.
   3. Martha served a banquet for Jesus here.
   2. Where Jesus wept
   1. People flocked to this town to see Jesus—and Lazarus, back from the dead.

C. 5. There were delicious fish there and wonderful cucumbers, melons, leeks, onions, and garlic.
   4. Hagar's homeland
   3. Scene of the first Passover
   2. Jeremiah was forced to flee there.
   1. Joseph's family settled in the region of Goshen in this country.

D. 5. Town where a paralyzed man went through the roof
   4. Jesus said Sodom would have repented if it had seen the miracles he was doing in this town.
   3. The disciples were rowing toward this city when they saw Jesus walking on the water.
   2. Town where Jesus healed Peter's mother-in-law
   1. Jesus moved to this town on the shores of Galilee early in his ministry.

E. 5. Jebus
   4. During Solomon's reign, "silver was as common as stones" in this city.
   3. Don't swear by this city.
   2. Jesus told the disciples to stay there until the Holy Spirit came upon them.
   1. The psalmist asks that we pray for this city's peace.

F. 5. Abraham recovered the plunder taken from this city.
   4. Kedorlaomer plundered this city and took Lot hostage.
   3. Lot's lot
   2. "Flee for your lives," the angels told Lot's family as they ran out of this city. "And don't look back!"
   1. Lot's wife looked back at the fire and flaming tar God sent upon this city—and she was a-salt-ed.

G. 5. Jerusalem's older sister, according to Ezekiel
   4. James and John wanted to call down fire from heaven on a noncooperative village in this area.
   3. Where Simon tried to buy the power of the Holy Spirit
   2. People from this region worshiped at Mount Gerizim, the woman told Jesus at the well.
   1. Usually Jews wouldn't speak to people from this region.

H. 5. Eleven days by foot from Kadesh-barnea

Places (cont.)

4. Where Elijah heard God in a gentle whisper
3. Where God wrote in stone
2. Where Aaron said, "Give me your gold earrings."
1. Moses was there receiving God's law for 40 days and 40 nights.

I. 5. King Ahaz saw an altar he liked in this city and sent a sketch back to Jerusalem.
4. Paul met a believer named Ananias here and had an enlightening experience.
3. Naaman the leper washed in the Jordan, but he preferred the rivers of this city.

2. Paul was let down the wall of this city in a basket.
1. On the road to this city, Paul was converted.

J. 5. Its reconstruction was completed in the sixth year of King Darius II.
4. Where Peter and John healed a man lame from birth
3. Where Jesus saw a widow donate two copper coins
2. Where a curtain (veil) split from top to bottom when Jesus died
1. The Lord told David not to build this.

STEP QUIZZES

14

Things, etc.

This category includes objects, food, plants, and animals.

A. 5. If the people had been indoors, would these things have been served on multiplication tables?
4. Andrew found a youngster with this food and introduced him to Jesus.
3. After Jesus worked a miracle with these things, the well-fed crowd wanted to make him king.
2. Jesus told his disciples to feed the crowd, but this was all the food they could find.
1. Jesus fed 5,000 men with these.

B. 5. God asked Moses, "What do you have there in your hand?" What was it?
4. Moses threw it on the ground and then ran away from it.
3. Moses parted with it.
2. Aaron and Hur helped Moses hold this up in the air so Israel would win the battle.
1. Twice, Moses struck rocks with this, and water gushed out.

C. 5. This tree's fruit was lovely and fresh looking.
4. The fruit of its fruit was death.
3. Eden's untouchable
2. The serpent told Eve that the fruit of this tree would make her to be like God.
1. Adam was forbidden to eat this tree's fruit.

D. 5. Colorful gift wrap
4. When Jacob saw this bloodred, he was blue.
3. After taking this from Joseph, Joseph's brothers sold him for silver.
2. Jacob's other sons were green with envy over this garment.

1. Because Joseph was the son he had when he was old and gray, Jacob gave him this special gift.

E. 5. In Revelation, when John ate a scroll, it tasted like this, but it still gave him indigestion.
4. In Samson's riddle, this was the "food [that] came out of the eater" and the "sweetness from the strong."
3. In Psalm 19, the psalmist calls God's laws sweeter than this.
2. John the Baptist ate this with locusts.
1. Besides milk, what the Promised Land flowed with

F. 5. Feed bin where sin was done in
4. An angel told shepherds they'd find their Savior lying there.
3. Christ's cradle
2. Bed for the Bethlehem baby
1. Mary had to put Jesus here because there was no room in the inn.

G. 5. Giant-killer's weapon
4. How Goliath got stoned
3. A shepherd boy conquered the Philistine champion with this weapon.
2. David picked up five smooth stones to use with this.
1. What David used to fell Goliath

H. 5. The emperor's image was on this.
4. Jesus told Peter to catch a fish and look in its mouth. What would he find?
3. Jesus told of a woman who lost one of these and swept every nook and cranny until she found it.

Things, etc. (cont.)

2. When asked whether it was right to pay taxes to Rome, Jesus asked to see this.
1. Jesus was watching the rich give their offerings in the temple when a poor widow came by and gave two of these.

I.
5. Golden earrings, melted down and remolded
4. In anger, Moses melted this in fire, ground it to powder, and mixed it into the drinking water.
3. At Sinai, the people exclaimed, "O Israel, this is the god that brought you out of Egypt!" What were they referring to?

2. Explaining how he made this, Aaron said, "Well, I told them, 'Bring me your gold earrings.' So they brought them to me and I threw them into the fire and . . . well . . . this . . . came out!"
1. When Moses saw this idol, he smashed the stone tablets that contained the Ten Commandments.

J.
5. 450 feet by 75 feet by 45 feet
4. It came to rest on Ararat.
3. How Shem, Ham, Japheth, their wives, and their parents escaped drowning
2. Floating zoo
1. Noah built it for a rainy day—and then some.

STEP QUIZZES

15

Things, etc.

A. 5. Error darer
   4. God said that this creature would always be an enemy of woman.
   3. This thing hissed, "That's a lie! You'll not die!"
   2. The craftiest creature in Eden
   1. This creature tricked Eve into the first sin.

B. 5. Eventually, Samson was bound with bronze chains but without this.
   4. So long, Samson's strength
   3. Cut by a Philistine barber
   2. Samson told Delilah he could be captured if she wove this into her loom. He lied.
   1. The secret of Samson's strength

C. 5. Hot rod to heaven?
   4. This separated Elisha and Elijah for the last time.
   3. Elisha called this "The Chariot of Israel."
   2. This vehicle was drawn by horses of fire.
   1. Elijah was carried to heaven in a whirlwind, not this, though this vehicle was on the scene.

D. 5. Nailed to this was a signboard in three languages.
   4. In Colossians, Paul pictures God taking a list of your sins and nailing them to this.
   3. Simon of Cyrene was forced to carry this.
   2. Joseph took Jesus down from here.
   1. Instrument of Jesus' death—and our life

E. 5. Before Philip found him, Nathanael was under one of these.
   4. James says you can't get olives from this.
   3. "Never bear fruit again!" Jesus told one of these.
   2. Jesus' attempt to satisfy his hunger here was fruitless.
   1. It withered after Jesus cursed it.

F. 5. This was placed in the ark of the covenant as a reminder of Korah's rebellion.
   4. This ate the "magic wands" of Pharaoh's magicians.
   3. Snake stake, for Pharaoh's sake
   2. When Aaron hit the dust with this, the land was laced with lice.
   1. This blooming thing proved that Aaron was God's chosen.

G. 5. According to the psalmist, it was angel food cake.
   4. Wonder bread
   3. The name means, "What is it?" because the Israelites saw it covering the ground and wondered.
   2. The Israelites made pancakes from this.
   1. White and flat, it tasted like honey bread.

H. 5. As Jesus saw it, this creature symbolized Jesus' own tomb.
   4. Prophet-taking sea creature
   3. It got sick of Jonah.
   2. Where Jonah prayed, "O Lord my God, you have snatched me from the yawning jaws of death."
   1. Jonah spent three days and nights in this.

Things, etc. (cont.)

I. 5. When asked why they were taking this animal, the disciples simply said, "The Lord needs him!"
   4. Jesus was the first to ride it.
   3. Palm plodder
   2. Zechariah predicted that the Lord would ride an animal like this—as Jesus did, several days before his death.
   1. Transport for the Triumphal Entry

J. 5. Broken laws?
   4. The Lord told Moses to take two of these and call him in the morning.
   3. God wrote on these himself.
   2. In anger at the Israelites' idolatry and immorality, Moses dashed these to the ground and broke them.
   1. Where God wrote the Ten Commandments

STEP QUIZZES

16

Things, etc.

A. 5. The hottest place in Babylon
   4. For three Hebrew youths, this was heated up seven times hotter than usual.
   3. Nebuchadnezzar's men threw three men into this, but the king saw four.
   2. Where Shadrach and friends found flame fame
   1. What God delivered Shadrach, Meshach, and Abednego from, unsinged

B. 5. Gideon gave it dew consideration.
   4. The first night, Gideon asked God to make this thing wet with dew but to keep the ground dry around it.
   3. Unsatisfied with one miracle, Gideon placed this outside a second night—to make sure God wasn't pulling the wool over his eyes.
   2. Sheepishly, Gideon asked God to do a second miracle: Put dew on the ground but not on this.
   1. To determine whether God really wanted him to lead Israel, Gideon placed this outside on the ground overnight.

C. 5. When Peter was told, *"This* is my beloved Son, and I am wonderfully pleased with him. Obey *him,"* this is where the voice came from.
   4. Israel's night-light
   3. This covered the tabernacle when the glory of the Lord filled it.
   2. This covered Mount Sinai when Moses was up there.
   1. In the wilderness, when this moved, the Israelites moved, too.

D. 5. The very night this appeared, Darius the Mede crashed Belshazzar's party.
   4. *Mene Mene Tekel Parsin*
   3. Wall scrawl
   2. When Belshazzar saw this, his knees knocked with fear.
   1. Daniel read this for King Belshazzar and proclaimed that God was sending judgment on Babylon.

E. 5. When Elisha decided to give up farming for prophecy, he used wood from this to build a fire and roast his oxen.
   4. Melt this into swords, says Joel.
   3. Micah says people will beat their swords into these.
   2. Elisha, when we first read of him, is the twelfth of 12 in a field pushing these.
   1. Farm tool that Elisha was pushing when Elijah found him

F. 5. Borrowed tool lost in the flow, but then it turned up
   4. While a seminary student was chopping wood, this fell into the river.
   3. Elisha had to recover this thing miraculously so the seminarians could chop wood for a new dormitory.
   2. At the cutting edge of prophetic ministry, Elisha restored the seminary's sinking fortunes by making this rise to the top.
   1. Elisha threw a stick into the Jordan and made this tool reappear.

Things, etc. (cont.)

G. 5. Bezalel's box
   4. 3¾ feet by 2¼ feet by 2¼ feet of acacia wood
   3. David danced before the Lord with all his might as he brought this holy thing to Jerusalem.
   2. When the Philistines put this Israelite treasure chest in the temple of their idol Dagon, the idol fell facedown before it.
   1. On the lid of this holy box were two statues of angels.

H. 5. In Revelation, this part of the attacking locusts sounded like chariots rushing into battle.
   4. Malachi says the Sun of Righteousness will rise with healing in these.
   3. Jesus said he wanted to gather Jerusalem's children as a mother hen gathers chicks beneath these.
   2. The angels Isaiah saw around God's throne each had six of these.
   1. Those who wait on the Lord will mount up with these like eagles.

I. 5. Tobiah teased that if a fox walked along the top of these, they would collapse.
   4. The new ones will be 1500 miles high and 216 feet thick, as the angel measured it.
   3. From here, people of Jerusalem listened to the demands of the Assyrians' envoy to Hezekiah.
   2. The Chaldean army tore these down.
   1. Nehemiah says it took only 52 days to rebuild them.

J. 5. After presenting these gifts, the givers were warned in a dream to change their travel plans.
   4. What the stargazers gave
   3. In a house in Bethlehem, foreigners bowed and presented these items to a child.
   2. Birthday gifts for a newborn king
   1. Visitors from the east brought these exotic presents to Bethlehem.

LOGIC PROBLEMS

Follow the instructions for each puzzle.

The best way to solve these is to make a chart. If you have five characters with five different things for five different occasions, you'll need three 5-by-5 box charts: characters to things, characters to occasions, things to occasions. (If you have four things to solve for, you'll need six charts.)

Then go through the clues. If you are told anything straight out (Abraham has the brown tent), circle the space where Abraham's line intersects the brown tent line—*and X out all the other spaces for both Abraham and the brown tent.*

Look for negative statements as well. If you're told Isaac did not use the black tent, then you can X out the appropriate space.

Use the process of elimination. If you're told the white tent was used by a woman, you can X out Abraham, Isaac, and Jacob—though you still don't know whether it was Sarah or Rebekah.

Keep checking the chart to see if you've X'd out all other possibilities for someone. If Sarah has X's for the black, brown, blue, and red tent, she must have the white tent.

Once you've made a match, make sure to match up the boxes with regard to the third thing. That is, if Abraham has the brown tent, and you're told that the brown tent user did not go to Egypt, cross the river, or meet the king—then you know those same facts apply to Abraham, and you can X out his boxes accordingly.

Keep going back through all these tips. With every finding, the logical situation changes. Through elimination, one clue may give you three others.

LOGIC PROBLEMS

1

Animals

We're in heaven, and—wouldn't you know it?—five Bible characters brought pets. David brought a lamb, Daniel a lion. Elijah brought the raven that fed him by the brook, and Moses brought the snake he lifted up in the wilderness (John 3:14). And of course Balaam (don't ask how he got here!) brought his talking donkey.

But once they got there, they decided to trade their pets, so that none of them ended up with the one he started with. And, oh yes, each pet has been given a name. From the clues provided, can you figure out which character ended up with each pet, and what each pet was named?

1. The lamb and the snake have names that begin with the same letter.

2. Elijah now has the pet named Hank.

3. Moses and Balaam have the pets that are not four-legged.

4. The lion and the lamb now belong to two people whose names begin with the same letter.

5. If the pets' names were listed in alphabetical order, the raven's name would come immediately before the donkey's.

6. Felicia does not slither.

7. If the pet-owners' names were listed alphabetically, Buddy's owner would come immediately before Brenda's.

8. The lion and the lamb have names with the same number of letters as their owners' names.

9. Roger is not the raven.

_____

_____

_____

_____

LOGIC PROBLEMS

2

2 Kings

Elisha seems to have led a group called "the company of the prophets." This may have been some sort of seminary for prophets-in-training. (That much is true. The rest of this puzzle? Well, you decide.) According to a spurious ancient document discovered in a dryer at a New Jersey laundromat, five of these seminarians were sent to five different places in Israel, where each performed a different miracle—with mixed results. Your job . . . to match up the person to the place and the miracle.

1. The one who went to Bethel made a hammer fly—though some say it just slipped out of his hand.

2. Abigail and Miriam were the only two women in this group. One of them went to a mountain.

3. One person went to Mt. Tabor, but it wasn't Simon or Marcus.

4. After a long drought, one of them called lightning from the sky and then recuperated in a place that did not begin with a B.

5. Someone whose name began with an M healed a stomachache by inventing an early form of Alka-Seltzer.

6. Simon did not go to Jezreel or Bethany.

7. One of the men made a baby stop crying by standing on his head. His own head, not the baby's.

8. The person who went to Mt. Gerizim helped a poor widow by giving her an unending supply of asparagus.

9. Neither of those who went to mountains had a name beginning with M.

10. The person who went to Mt. Tabor has a name beginning with a consonant.

11. Frodo was not the one who called lightning from the sky.

12. No women were sent to any place beginning with a B.

LOGIC PROBLEMS

1 Chronicles

Five men sang in a heavenly quintet. All are named in 1 Chronicles 1:1–2:4. Two sing baritone, two sing tenor, one sings bass. Each is working on a different solo for the big Christmas concert. Can you match the person with the part he sings and the song he sings?

The following clues, along with the text of 1 Chronicles 1:1–2:4, will help.

1. There are two, and only two, father-son pairs in the group.

2. The son of Lamech is the only one to sing in his part.

3. Japheth is not one of the five group members.

4. Methusaleh's great-grandson sings "O Come All Ye Faithful."

5. A tenor sings "Silent Night."

6. Neither Canaan nor his father or sons are included in the group.

7. The one who sings "Angels We Have Heard on High" had eleven brothers and five sons.

8. The ones who sing "O Come All Ye Faithful" and "Joy to the World" sing the same part.

9. Only one of the tenors has his father in the group.

10. Abraham's grandson sings "Silent Night."

11. Isaac is in the group—but it's someone else who sings "Hark the Herald."

LOGIC PROBLEMS

4

Job

Years after the events of the book of Job (according to the story we're making up for this puzzle), Job got together again with his old pals—Eliphaz, Zophar, Elihu, and Bildad. Each of them, to their surprise, wore a tattoo that reminded them of something God had said at the end of the book—a raven, a lion, an ostrich, a behemoth, and Leviathan. Job took the occasion to give each of his friends a gift from the plenty that God had restored to him. These gifts were a camel, a gold ring, a silver piece, and a yoke of oxen.

Now, what tattoo did each of the five men wear? And what gifts did Job give to each of his four friends? (NOTE: Job himself received no gift.)

1. A gold ring was given to the man who wore the tattoo of Leviathan.

2. The beast mentioned in Job 40:15 was tattooed on someone, but it wasn't Job or Zophar.

3. The two men whose names started with the same letter received a yoke of oxen and a camel.

4. The first man to address Job in the book of Job wore a raven tattoo.

5. The beast mentioned in Job 38:39 was tattooed on someone, but not on the one who received the silver piece or the camel.

6. Zophar did not receive the gold ring.

7. One of the men wearing a tattoo of a bird has a name that begins with the last letter of the name of the other man wearing a bird tattoo.

8. The man wearing the behemoth tattoo received the camel as a gift.

_____

_____

_____

_____

LOGIC PROBLEMS

5

Psalms

A heavenly combo has convened. Two women, Anna and Deborah, have joined with three male biblical characters to play selections from the psalms. Each plays a different instrument (one of these is a lyre), and each one plays a solo on a particular psalm. The five psalms they play are numbered 1, 19, 42, 103, 119 (at least in the Protestant psalter). You may need to look these up to decipher some clues.

Which instrument does each character play, and which psalm does each play a solo on?

1. Barnabas solos on the psalm that starts "Praise the Lord" (or, "Bless the Lord," in some versions).

2. It's a man who solos on the psalm that begins, "The heavens declare the glory of God."

3. The harpist is featured on a psalm whose number has two digits.

4. Deborah solos on a psalm whose number has three digits.

5. Caleb's solo psalm has the fewest verses.

6. One of the women plays the harp. The other plays the high-sounding cymbals.

7. They perform these five psalms in numerical order, beginning with Psalm 1 and ending with Psalm 119. Ehud's solo psalm comes immediately after the one that features the low-sounding cymbals.

8. The trumpet solo comes somewhere before Barnabas's solo in the program.

_____

_____

_____

_____

_____

_____

LOGIC PROBLEMS

6

Daniel

Dr. Milton Digman has spent most of his life underground. Good thing. This mad archaeologist has come up with a theory about Daniel in ancient Persia. Piecing together bits of evidence from ancient tablets, Digman suggests that Daniel and his three friends—Shadrach, Meshach, and Abednego—were each given a number of cities to rule. One ruled four cities; another, three; another, two; and the other, one. Each had his capital in a different Persian city or region. And you may remember from chapter 1 of Daniel that these four ate vegetables instead of the king's rich meat. Digman says that each of the four had a favorite vegetable. In addition, each of them suffered a major catastrophe.

Digman offers the following clues from the ancient scrolls. Maybe you can figure them out. For each of the four princes, you need to find out (a) how many cities he ruled; (b) where his capital was; (c) what vegetable he liked; and (d) what catastrophe befell him. This is the hardest logic puzzler in the book, so sharpen your pencil and go to it.

1. The one who ruled three cities was based in Susa.

2. Abednego ruled one more city than Meshach did.

3. The lima-bean lover was nearly strangled by the hanging gardens.

4. One of them had carvings of his loved ones burned in the fiery furnace, but it wasn't Daniel.

5. The one whose capital was Susa lost his appointment book and missed the annual croquet game with the other princes.

6. The one who ruled the most cities enjoyed spinach the most.

7. One of them had a nervous breakdown after dreaming about himself interpreting his own dream. This person ruled one less city than the one who preferred broccoli.

8. One of them liked okra, but it wasn't Meshach or Daniel.

9. Only one of the four was based in a city that starts in the same letter as his name.

10. Elam and Media were two of the capitals, but neither was home base to the broccoli lover.

11. The one based in Ur loved okra.

12. Neither Shadrach nor Meshach liked broccoli.

_____

_____

_____

_____

_____

_____

_____

_____

_____

_____

_____

_____

_____

_____

_____

_____

_____

_____

_____

_____

_____

_____

Micah

Micah 4 talks about beating swords into plowshares and about "every man" sitting "under his fig tree." But part-time Bible scholar (and part-time pro wrestler) Wolfgang "Hunk" Humdinger has a new theory. He suggests that Micah had four friends, each of whom had a different weapon that he or she beat into a different farm implement. Each one also sat under a different kind of tree.

Put the person with the weapon he or she started with, the tool it became, and the type of tree the person sat under.

1. Obviously, the one who sat under the fig tree beat his sword into a plowshare.

2. Darla had nothing to do with the sword, spear, or sickel.

3. The one who sat under the date tree ended up with a hoe.

4. The one who started with a shield sat under a plum tree.

5. The arrows were beaten into back scratchers.

6. Somebody sat under a juniper tree, but it wasn't Abel or Benjamin.

7. Cyrus did not end up with the hoe or plowshare.

8. The one who started with a spear had a name that began with a consonant.

_____

_____

_____

_____

_____

_____

_____

_____

LOGIC PROBLEMS

Zechariah

Zechariah saw a vision (Zech. 4) of seven lamps on a lampstand. Each was connected by a pipe to a bowl of oil, which was supplied by two olive trees. Well, we've played with this picture a bit. Let's say each of the lamps bears a different name—in honor of the promised Messiah. The names are "Branch," "Son of Man," "Ancient of Days," "Root," "Ruler," "Prince of Peace," and "Sun of Righteousness."

In addition, each of the pipes is made of a different metal—gold, silver, bronze, zinc, iron, copper, and tin. Each pipe connects with one of the two trees—either the right one or the left one. See if you can determine which metal made up the pipe leading to which lamp, and which of the two trees it got its oil from.

1. The gold pipe leads to the lamp that gets its name from Zechariah 6:12.

2. The olive tree on the left supplies three of the lamps.

3. The silver and tin pipes lead to lamps whose names begin with the same letter. Those two pipes also hook up to the same tree.

4. There are two lamps that get their names from Daniel 7:13. These are connected to two pipes whose metals are mentioned in Daniel 2:32.

5. Two of the pipes leading from the left tree are copper and zinc.

6. The lamp whose name comes from Isaiah 9:6 is hooked up to the same tree that supplies the iron pipe.

7. The names of the lamps supplied by the copper and zinc pipes begin with different letters.

8. The lamp named Ruler is supplied by a pipe whose metal also ends with an R.

Those clues should be enough. But if you need more, here they are.

9. Only one name starts with a vowel. Its lamp is hooked up to the tree on the right.

10. The lamps named Branch and Root are hooked up to different trees.

11. The lamp whose name comes from Micah 5:2 is connected to a different tree from the one that supplies the bronze pipe.

12. Of the lamps named Ancient of Days, Ruler, and Prince of Peace, only one hooks up to the tree on the right.

_____

_____

_____

_____

_____

_____

_____

_____

_____

_____

_____

_____

_____

_____

_____

_____

_____

_____

_____

_____

_____

_____

LOGIC PROBLEMS

9

Romans

According to a dubious first-century document, when Paul sent his epistle to the Romans, he also sent gifts to six members of the church there—six different gifts from six different places to six of the people in Rome. And to test their intellectual prowess, he gave strange clues about who would receive what gift.

You need to figure out *which gift* from *which place* was given to *which person*. You will need to consult Romans 16 for some details about the people involved. (You may also need a table of contents of the New Testament.)

1. There were two gifts that might be considered medicinal. These came from Laodicea and Philippi.

2. There were two gifts from places Paul did not address epistles to. These gifts both went to men.

3. The camel whip went to someone to whom "all the churches of the Gentiles are grateful."

4. The gift from Philippi went to one who had "worked very hard."

5. The gift of parchment came from Ephesus.

6. Paul gave nothing to a woman he said was "a mother to me." But he gave some eye salve to her son.

7. Persis got the cloak.

8. Priscilla's gift and Mary's gift both came from places that received New Testament epistles. In fact, these epistles appear back to back (Priscilla's first).

9. The person from Cenchrea did not receive the gift from Colosse, but from another city beginning with a C.

10. There were two items of clothing given. Both went to women whose names began with P.

11. The toga did not come from Damascus, but another gift did.

12. The olive oil did not come from Corinth, but another gift did.

Biblical Clues

A. Paul wrote epistles to Rome, Corinth, Galatia, Ephesus, Philippi, Colosse, and Thessalonica.

B. Of the people named in Romans 16, Aquila, Epenetus, Andronicus, Urbanus, Apelles, and others are male. Tryphena, Tryphosa, Persis, and others are female. Any other names you need are what you would expect, still common as male or female names today.

C. Olive oil was used for medicinal purposes.

_____

_____

_____

_____

_____

_____

_____

_____

_____

_____

_____

_____

_____

_____

_____

_____

_____

71

LOGIC PROBLEMS

Philemon

Paul asked Philemon to keep a guest room ready for him. So what happened when he finally did show up? Was the runaway slave Onesimus with him? This logic problem supposes that five people did stay in Philemon's house one night—Philemon and his wife, Apphia, their son Archippus, Paul, and Onesimus. (Scholars really do think that Apphia was Philemon's wife, and Archippus may have been their son.) You should also note that Paul called Onesimus "my son," spiritually speaking, in verse 10. (For the purposes of this puzzle, assume that Onesimus is the only person that Paul would call "son.")

Anyway, this problem suggests that the five people stayed in five different rooms, each of a different color. And each did something different before retiring for the night. Match the person to the activity and the color of the room.

1. The purple room went to someone whose name began with P.

2. One person read the letters of Paul before retiring for the night, but it wasn't Paul.

3. The person in the brown room was male.

4. The person who prayed before retiring and the person who sang a song of praise had names that began with the same letter.

5. The person in the white room did some reading.

6. One person read from the Old Testament, but it wasn't Apphia or her husband.

7. The person who read from the Gospels was not in the scarlet room.

8. Archippus did not read.

9. The person in the gray room was not Onesimus.

10. The scarlet room housed the person who read Paul's epistles.

11. Paul did not read from the Gospels that night.

12. "Goodnight, my son," said the person in the white room to the person who prayed before bed.

LOGIC PROBLEMS

11

Revelation

The Book of Revelation was written to seven churches of Asia Minor. In chapters 2 and 3, each church is addressed directly, with special affirmations and criticisms. Church historian Weldon Weisgeis of Ahman Lubwith University. has theorized that each of these churches chose a different Old Testament book to read from when it welcomed new members. Also, in a more controversial theory, Weisgeis says that each church followed its dedication service with a different activity.

Weisgeis developed his thesis only after poring over the ancient evidence, devoting his full attention to the archaeological clues. It took him at least twenty minutes. Let's see how long it takes you.

You need to figure out *which church* read *which book* and did *which activity*. You will need to consult Revelation 2–3 for information about the seven churches (and perhaps a table of contents for the whole Bible).

1. The church that read from Proverbs finished its service with an ancient form of bowling.

2. The first two churches addressed in Revelation read from back-to-back books of the Old Testament.

3. One of the churches followed its service by eating dessert, but it wasn't the one that read from Job.

4. Word games were the after-church activity of one of the churches whose location started with the letter P.

5. Isaiah and Jeremiah were two of the books read, but not by the churches that enjoyed chariot races or eating dessert.

6. The churches that read from Genesis and Proverbs were located in cities that started with the same letter.

7. The church that was promised a "white stone" spent its after-church hours sleeping.

8. Joshua was the book read by the church that was addressed right after the one that played word games.

9. Appropriately, the church that read from the Psalms also enjoyed singing afterward.

10. The church that engaged in archery read from a book that started with the letter J.

11. The church in Philadelphia read from a book that immediately precedes the book read by the church that had "forsaken its first love."

12. The church that "tolerated Jezebel" did not read from Isaiah.

13. The book read by the dessert-eating church comes somewhere after (but not immediately after) the book read by the chariot-racing church.

Section 2

travel games

TRAVEL GAMES

Where Are We Going?

Start by asking the family questions about the trip you're on.

Where are we going?
How will we travel?
What are we taking?
How far are we going?
Where will we stay when we get there (or along the way)?

Now choose a Bible character who went on a journey. See if you can answer the same questions for that character. Feel free to use a Bible to get the info you need.

Consider the following biblical travelers:

- Jacob traveling back to Canaan (Gen. 31–33)
- Joseph sold as a slave to Egypt (Gen. 37:25, 36)
- The Israelites in the wilderness (Exod., Num.)
- David going to join his brothers (1 Sam. 17:17-20)
- The queen of Sheba traveling to see King Solomon (1 Kings 10:1-9)
- Elijah running away from Queen Jezebel (1 Kings 19:1-5)
- The Israelites returning from Babylonian captivity (Ezra, Neh.)

- Mary and Joseph going to Bethlehem (Luke 2:4-5)
- Mary and Joseph fleeing to Egypt (Matt. 2:13-15; see also 2:19-23)
- The man who was helped by the Good Samaritan (Luke 10:30-35)
- The Ethiopian ruler who was met by Philip (Acts 8:26-40)
- Paul and Barnabas setting out on their first missionary journey (Acts 13:1-5)
- Paul heading for Rome on his last journey (Acts 27–28)

We don't know all the answers for each of these Bible stories, but you can guess. Compare the biblical journeys to your own.

License Lessons

Using the letters on license plates again, see if you can form a simple sentence that expresses a Bible truth. This time PAB might stand for "Put Away Bickering" (which might be an appropriate lesson for a carful of youngsters).

TRAVEL GAMES

A Car of a Different Color

Look at another car on the road—what color is it? Try to think of something in the Bible of the same color. Rahab's scarlet cord, the "green pastures" of Psalm 23, or even the Red Sea. Be creative with this. Was David feeling "blue" when he wrote certain psalms? And did the zebra on Noah's ark have black stripes, or were the stripes white?

Still, you can't repeat a biblical reference. If you see a second car of the same color, you have to think up a new thing from the Bible.

License to Spell

Look for the letters on the license plates of cars around you. See if you can come up with Bible names that start with each letter on the license plate. Extra credit if the Bible names are related to each other in some way. (PAB might be Paul and Barnabas, who traveled from Antioch.)

Signs of the Times

Look for road signs that have a Bible connection. This could be one of those ongoing games that's carried through a whole trip. Assign one, three, or five points for each connection made, depending on how good it is, and let the players keep their own tallies throughout the trip.

Examples: "STOP sinning" is probably worth one point. But "YIELD not to temptation" might get you three. If you see a Holiday Inn and comment about the inn that had no room for Joseph and Mary, that's great. Even more so if you note that Christmas is a "holiday." (If you see a No Vacancy sign, so much the better.) And of course if you're passing by Zion, Illinois, or Bethlehem, Pennsylvania, you're in fine shape.

TRAVEL GAMES

———————————— ■ ————————————

Dream Team

Sports teams are often named for birds, animals, or certain types of people. But what if certain Bible characters had teams—what would they be called? You can all have fun with this. Goliath's team would be, of course, the Giants. David (the shepherd) might manage the Rams (and lead them against the Bears and the Lions). John the Baptist would surely be on the Trailblazers. You get the idea.

Consider making up new team names. Noah might lead the Arkies or the Floaters. Peter might start the Waterwalkers. And so on.

———————————— ■ ————————————

Star Search

This game requires two people, a pencil, and paper. It is just like Hangman (but less violent) and something like *Wheel of Fortune.* One person is the Giver, who thinks up the name of a Bible character, place, or thing—or perhaps a short Bible verse. The Giver then draws blank spaces on the paper, one for each letter, leaving space between words. So "John the Baptist" would look like:

—— —— —— —— —— —— —— —— —— —— —— —— —— ——

Then the Giver tells the Guesser what category he has chosen (person, place, thing, or verse), and the Guesser begins to guess letters that might be in it. If she guesses an *A,* the Giver writes in all the *A's* in the puzzle, and so on. If there are none of that letter, the Giver draws one stroke of a five-pointed star. After five wrong guesses, the star will be completed, and the Guesser loses. At any time, the Guesser can solve the puzzle.

Options: You could limit the guesses to consonants, and give the Guesser the chance to "buy" vowels one at a time *(A, E, I, O, U,* not *Y).* Buying a vowel would mean adding a stroke to the star, but you do get to see the vowels in the puzzle.

You could have two or three Guessers playing at the same time, taking turns with guesses.

If the five-pointed star is too tough, try a six-pointed Star of David (two overlapping triangles).

80

TRAVEL GAMES

Memory Chain

Player 1 says, "If we could be Bible characters, I'd be Abigail" (or any name beginning with *A*).

Player 2 says, "If we could be Bible characters, you'd be Abigail, I'd be Barnabas" (or any name beginning with *B*).

Player 3 says, "If we could be Bible characters, you'd be Abigail, you'd be Barnabas, I'd be Caleb" (or any name beginning with *C*). And so on, around the circle. If someone forgets a name, start over.

You can always skip the letters *Q*, *W*, and *X* (but think about "queen of Sheba" or "witch of Endor" as possibilities).

After trying this with Bible characters, you could try again with Bible things.

Numbers and Colors

For younger children, this can be a good observation game. First, think of a Bible story that has both a number and a color. Then ask the players to look for that number of things that are that color.

Examples: Moses held *two* hands up at the *Red* Sea. Find two things that are red.

When Jesus left, the *eleven* remaining disciples were *blue*. Find eleven things that are blue.

Peter denied Christ *three* times because he was *yellow*. Find three things that are yellow.

What's Missing?

All you need for this game is a Bible. Read a verse (of 10 to 20 words), but leave one word out. See if the players can guess the missing word.

Be ready to give clues—other meanings, the letter it starts with, the first (or last) syllable, or a word it rhymes with.

This can be as easy or difficult as you choose because you can pick familiar verses or obscure ones.

TRAVEL GAMES

■

Sound FX

Think about the sounds of certain biblical events. Try to produce these sounds and have the others guess the event. You may need to give clues: Who was involved? What objects were present? What had happened previously?

Examples: The sound of God creating the elephant. The sound of Miriam playing tambourine as the Egyptian army was swept away by the Red Sea. The sound of Elijah calling fire from heaven to consume his sacrifice. The sound of David slinging a stone at Goliath. The sound of the rooster crowing and Peter weeping.

■

Billboard Blast

Look for a billboard with a simple message of up to 10 words. Then, have some fun taking the *initials* of the words of that message and making up a sentence involving Bible characters with those same initials. So, "Coke refreshes like no other soft drink" could result in "Cain refused, leaving Noah outside, scrubbing donkeys." Notice that the sentences don't have to be biblically correct. They can be funny, but they have to use Bible characters.

■

Bible Book Bash

Take the initials of the books of the Bible, in order, and create some silly sentences with those same initials. Genesis, Exodus, Leviticus, and so on, could become "Go eat loose nails, doing jumping jacks rightly. . . ." (Use *F* and *S* for First and Second books, or use the *S* of Samuel twice and the *K* of Kings twice, and so on.) You could also start with the New Testament books. This can be a lot of fun and a good way to learn the order of Bible books.

TRAVEL GAMES

Sing the Psalms

If you have a musical family, this one's for you. The book of Psalms was written to be sung. Obviously, we don't have the music that the Israelites originally used, but we can make up our own tunes.

Try it. Read a psalm together and then, verse by verse, try to sing it. You might take turns, with each family member taking one verse to sing. Start with familiar psalms, such as 1, 23, or 100. But then try some that might be new to you.

Do-It-Yourself Psalms

Make up your own psalms that tell God (and others) how you feel. We often think of the Psalms as pure praise, but there are some sad psalms, even some angry psalms. Read a few psalms to get the feel for how they were written, and choose one of the following themes:

- Sorry (like Ps. 51)
- Mad (like Pss. 36 or 52)
- Glad (like Pss. 30, 34, or 66)
- Sad (like Pss. 42, 43, or 54)
- Past things (like Ps. 136)
- Alphabetical (every verse starts with the same letter or with the next letter, like Pss. 111, 112, or 119 are in Hebrew)

Note that Psalms often uses *parallelism*. That is, the second line usually repeats the idea of the first. This can be a very educational technique. An adult or older child can make up the first line of each verse, and a younger child could say the same thing in different words.

If you come up with some good psalms, keep them and post them in your home.

TRAVEL GAMES

Soap Operas

Sometimes Bible stories can get as complicated as soap operas. Read these TV-like descriptions of Bible stories and see if people can guess what stories they are. Then make up your own descriptions of other stories.

1. Husband and wife have a happy home, until one sneaky character slithers in and convinces the wife to break the law. Then she gets her husband involved in the crime, and they both try to hide from the authorities.
2. Interracial couple faces problems because he won't tell her his secrets. He's a big man in town and uses his power against his enemies. But, after much pleading, he reveals his secret, and she betrays him, cutting off his power supply. She allows his enemies defeat him, but he gets his revenge and brings the whole operation crashing to the ground.
3. Unmarried woman finds that she is pregnant. But the man she is engaged to does not understand, since it is not his child. He threatens to disgrace her publicly, but then a strange visitor changes his mind. He accepts her, and they take a long trip together.
4. Big Man on Campus bullies everyone and taunts the opposing team as they prepare for the big matchup. The other team has no one that can stand up to him, and they're sure they will lose. But someone's kid brother decides he's heard enough. He doesn't even suit up—he's only a musician. But the kid gathers his rock band and launches his own challenge; that big bully is due for a fall. He gets rocked out of his mind, and the kid becomes a hero.
5. A young woman grieves over her dead husband, but her mother-in-law urges her to find a new man. Sure enough, there's an eligible single man in her field for whom she indicates her interest. He's interested, too, but has to complete a complex business deal before he can marry her. Will he succeed? Will they be wed? And what about Naomi?

(Answers are in the Answers section in the back of this book.)

Kids' Quiz

If the parents know the Bible pretty well, this could be a fun game. Using a Bible, the kids are to come up with a question that will stump their parents. Try reading a verse and asking the parents to guess what book it's from. (It would be easier if they read three or four verses from the same book.) Or find a character and ask a who question. Just leave the name out and ask, "Who did such and such?" (Warning: Stay away from lists of names in Numbers, 1 and 2 Chronicles, or the beginning of Matthew. No one knows that stuff.)

TRAVEL GAMES

Picnic

Player 1 begins by saying, "I'm going on a picnic, and I'm taking
. . ." Then, he adds two things, both starting with A: the name of
a Bible person and any food. For instance, "Adam's apple" or
"Benjamin's bread." Player 1 names things beginning with A,
Player 2 does B, and so on. (Especially with difficult letters, you
can stretch the rules. It doesn't have to be a name; it could be a
description, such as "the woman at the well" or "the queen of
Sheba." With X, you can use any name or word with an X in it.
And you might stretch the food to include any item you might
bring on a picnic.)

If you successfully get through the alphabet, add a new
element to the game: a place. Try to find a biblical place
beginning with the same letter. (Again, nonname descriptions are
acceptable, such as "the wilderness.") Now you'll say, "I'm going
on a trip, and I'm taking Adam's apple to Antioch." And so on.

I Spy

One player sees something, and the others have to guess what it
is. The player says, "I spy with my little eye something God made,
and it's _____" (any descriptive word can be given as a clue, such
as "green"). Other players then try to guess what it is. If no one
guesses the right thing, the player gives another clue for the same
object.

If you want to be a stickler for detail, stick with natural things
(things that "God made"), not cars, asphalt, and billboards, but
grass, trees, and clouds. Still, you might have a good opportunity
to teach how God made the minerals that went into the steel of
that car and that he made the people who built that car and so
on.

TRAVEL GAMES

Detective Prayers

As you travel, you will cross paths with many others, passing (or being passed) on the road, in the rest stops, motels, campgrounds, etc. Some will be in obvious need, like the occupants of a car stuck by the roadside. Others will seem to be having fun, just like you.

You can't always stop to help people in need, and you can't always get to know the people you pass. But you can pray for them, and this can be an instructional family exercise.

Put on your detective hats for a few minutes before you pray. What do you know about the people in that car you're passing? The license plate says Nebraska. What's it like in Nebraska, and why are they here? Are they at the end of their trip or the beginning? How many kids are there, and what are their ages? Do they look happy? What joys or needs might they have right now?

Based on your educated guesses about those people, pray for them. Certainly you don't need to pry into their lives. You're only guessing at things, and you'll probably never know what the truth of the matter is. But this is a good exercise for *you* to learn observation skills and to use what you've learned when you pray. Don't pray in a judgmental way but in a caring way. Don't say, "Lord, teach those lazy parents how to discipline their kids." Instead, you might say, "Lord, you know why those kids are behaving like that. Let there be peace in that family."

Theme Songs

How many Christian songs can you think of that have anything to do with travel? You may need to stretch this idea pretty far. "We Are Climbing Jacob's Ladder" might stretch to fit. And even "Amazing Grace" says, "I once was lost, but now am found."

TRAVEL GAMES

■

Song Spurs

Divide into two teams. Someone from Team A sees a word on a billboard or sign and shouts it out. Team B has to come up with a Christian song or hymn with that word in it. You have sixty seconds to get one, and you must sing at least six words of the song.

If Team B finds a song, then Team A gets a chance with the same word. If they succeed, play passes back to Team B. (Obviously, you can't repeat a song while dealing with the same word.) When a team fails, the other team gets a point—except on the first attempt. If the starting team fails, the other team must come up with a song in order to get a point. Otherwise, no point is awarded. Then you can go on to another billboard or sign.

■

Title Match

Think of titles of TV shows, movies, books, songs, and plays that might describe some biblical story or character. When one person thinks of one, he or she can name the title, and the others try to guess what Bible story fits. Or, try the reverse. Name the Bible story and give clues about what sort of title it is—"TV show, Tuesday night, starring Hank Heartthrob."

Examples: Wise Men's journey—"Star Trek"; Blind Man healed—"20/20"; David fleeing from Saul—"Who's the Boss?" or "The Fugitive."

TRAVEL GAMES

■

Twenty Questions

Create two teams. Team A decides on a person, story, or thing from the Bible. The other team asks up to 20 yes-or-no questions until they can guess what it is. (You may ask, "Was this person a king of Israel?" but not, "What country did this person live in?") And occasionally the answer will have to be "Sort of" or "In a way" or "Maybe." But try to stick to yeses and nos.

The guessing team gets one point for each guess (and the answer does count as a guess). Whichever team has the lowest point total wins.

Playing option: This can also be played with two individuals rather than teams.

Some suggested choices:

- *People:*
  Cain
  Methuselah
  Deborah
  Abigail
  Jonathan
  Malchus (the soldier
    who got his ear cut
    off by Peter)

- *Stories:*
  David killing Goliath
  the Tower of Babel
  the angels appearing
    to the shepherds
  Jesus feeding 5,000

- *Things:*
  Moses' staff
  David's sling
  fire from heaven (that
    consumed Elijah's
    sacrifice)
  Balaam's donkey
  Try to pin down the
    "thing" to a specific
    event in Scripture.
    For instance, say
    "manna" instead of
    simply "bread.")

Word Addition

The object of the game is to build sentences about Bible characters. Player 1 starts with a Bible character's name. Player 2 adds a word, any word, that might continue the sentence. Player 3 does the same, as do all the players (this is best for a large group, but you can play with as few as four—just keep rotating). Keep adding words into what may become a huge run-on sentence. When someone forgets a word in the sentence, you have to start over.

Example:
Player 1: Paul.
Player 2: Paul stood.
Player 3: Paul stood on.
Player 4: Paul stood on the.
Player 5: Paul stood on the mountain.
Player 6: Paul stood on the mountain, preaching.
Player 7: Paul stood on the mountain, preaching about.
Player 8: Paul stood on the mountain, preaching about good.
Player 9: Paul stood on the mountain, preaching about good things.
Player 10: Paul stood on the mountain, talking about good things and.
Player 6: You said "talking." It was "preaching."
Player 10: Aaauuuggghhh!
Player 11: Moses.
Player 12: Moses walked.
And so on.

∎

Random Reference

Look for license plates with combinations of letters and numbers. Take the first letter on the plate and see if you can name a book of the Bible that starts with that letter. Then see if you can put the numbers of the license plate together into a chapter-and-verse reference. Then look up that verse and read it out loud. For example, GN5 020 could mean Genesis 50:20, which reads, "As far as I am concerned, God turned into good what you meant for evil." (The random verses you come up with won't always be so wonderful, but you can also look at the context of the verse. In this case, it's Joseph reunited with his brothers, who had sold him into slavery.)

∎

Alphabuilding

Construct a paragraph in which each word starts with the next letter of the alphabet. Try to make it a Bible-related message of some kind. See if you can go from A to Z. After you've done it a few times, try starting with a different letter, or going backwards. For example, "Always Be Careful, Doing Everything Faithfully. Good Heavens! I Just Know Love Might Need One Person Questioning Right Solutions. The Unknown Varies While X-raying Your Zeal." (Don't ask what it means.)

This is a great game for groups of people. Go around a circle, with each person supplying the next word. One option: Allow a person to "pass" by supplying a punctuation mark instead of a word. ("Always Be Careful Doing Everything"—the next person can't think of an F, but says, "Period." Then the next one has to start a new sentence.) Another option: For Q, X, and Z, accept words that merely include the letter.

TRAVEL GAMES

───────────── ■ ─────────────

Back to the Billboard

You can't drive far nowadays without seeing a billboard hawking some product. Sometimes the ads are straightforward—"Eat at Joe's Diner." But sometimes they're misleading—"Be cool: drink Blarney Beer" (or something like that). The truth is, beer doesn't make you cool. As you read the billboards you pass, start talking back in biblical terms. "You Need This Car? I don't think so. You need to 'Love the Lord your God with all your heart, soul, and mind.'"

This might require some critical thinking that's beyond younger children, but it's not a bad idea to get them started on questioning the ads they see.

───────────── ■ ─────────────

Do-It-Yourself Parables

Jesus told parables based on the regular lives of the people around him. They were farmers and fishermen, merchants and beggars. He used the details of their everyday lives to express God's truth.

Why can't you tell a parable based on your life? Take some of Jesus' parables and try to retell them in your own terms. Maybe you're not buying a field with a treasure in it, but buying a box of Cracker Jack with a prize inside. Maybe you're not saving a lost sheep, but looking all over your house for your lost mittens.

You might consider the following parables:

The Prodigal Son (Luke 15:11-32)
The Good Samaritan (Luke 10:30-37)
The Sheep and the Goats (Matt. 25:31-46)
The Lost Sheep (Luke 15:4-7)
The Wheat and the Weeds (Matt. 13:24-30)
The Pearl of Great Price (Matt. 13:45-46)
The Talents (Matt. 25:14-30)
The Unforgiving Servant (Matt. 18:23-35)
Workers in the Vineyard (Matt. 20:1-16)
The Rich Man and Lazarus (Luke 16:19-31)

TRAVEL GAMES

∎

Acting the Part

One person chooses a Bible character and starts saying things that character might say. Others try to guess who it is. For example: "My, the view from up here is pretty good. I should climb sycamore trees more often, being as short as I am. Look, there's Jesus, and he's coming this way. What would he want with a tax collector like me?" (Zaccheus.)

∎

I Write the Songs

Take a song that everyone knows—some folk song, show tune, or TV theme song—and put new words to it, telling a Bible story or expressing a biblical theme. For instance, "Row, row, row your boat" could become:
Stow, stow, stow your boat
Fully with a flock
Of animals, animals, animals, animals—
Oops! I felt a drop.

∎

Bible Verse Giveaway

Find some favorite Bible verses and read them one by one. After each one, ask, "Who do we know that could use this verse?" You could pray, asking God to speak the message of those verses to those people. Or you could write down the verse and plan to send it to the people. The Psalms are great "giveaways" for this exercise, as well as some New Testament passages such as Romans 8 and 1 Corinthians 13.

TRAVEL GAMES

███

Bible Quality Giveaway

As you think of certain Bible characters and the qualities they showed, what qualities would you like to give to people you know? "I'd like to give Dad the courage of Daniel. I'd like to give Mom the faith of Hannah. I'd like to give Jason the wisdom of Solomon. I'd like to give Melissa the energy of David." You get the idea. A "game" like this can lead to prayers for all those people.

███

The Brightest and the Beast

This is a great imagination game for animal lovers. Think about some of the animals in the Bible, and then try to tell their stories from the animal's perspective. It may give you a whole new angle on these Bible events, and it'll be a lot of fun for everyone.
   Consider:

The raven or dove Noah sent from the ark (Gen. 8)
The ram Abraham sacrificed instead of Isaac (Gen. 22)
Balaam's donkey (Num. 22)
The sheep David was tending before he was anointed king (1 Sam. 16)
The raven that fed Elijah (1 Kings 17)
The lions that didn't eat Daniel (Dan. 6)
The great fish (or whale) that swallowed Jonah (Jon.1:17)
The sheep being tended when the angels announced Jesus' birth (Luke 2)
The donkey on which Jesus rode into Jerusalem (Matt. 21)
You could also reverse the process. Have a storyteller start talking from the animal's
   point of view while the others try to guess what story is being told.

███

Words, Words, Words

One person picks a favorite Bible verse. Another picks a number between 1 and 15. The first person has to summarize the meaning of the verse in that many words. For example, one person picks John 3:16, the other picks the number 7. So the verse is summarized in seven words: "God loved the world and sent Jesus."

TRAVEL GAMES

■

Two by Two

Sometimes people and things in the Bible come in pairs: Adam and Eve, James and John, loaves and fishes. Have everyone in the car write down five individual people or things in the Bible that belong to a pair. For instance, you might list Adam, John, loaves, Goliath, and First Corinthians. Then compare your lists. See if anyone else has the missing part of your pair (in this example, you'd be looking for Eve, James, fishes, David, or Second Corinthians). When a match is made, both people get a point. Then try again.

■

Bible Chain

Each person lists five Bible characters. Combine these lists into a master list of ten, fifteen, or twenty characters. Then try to find links between them, eventually including every character on your list. Look for family relationships first, but then there might be other connections. Be creative.

For example, your master list might look like this:

Moses
Esther
David
John
Paul
Miriam
Martha
Noah
Jonah
Eve

Then you'd start forging links. Paul quoted from Moses, who was the brother of Miriam. Like Miriam, Martha also had a brother. Like Martha, John was also a good friend of Jesus. John and David both wrote parts of the Bible. David and Esther were both royalty. Esther and Eve both have names beginning with E. Eve and Jonah both tried to hide from God. Jonah and Noah both had interesting experiences involving water.

TRAVEL GAMES

■

Top Ten

Try to come up with the top ten Bible people or things in different categories. Here are some suggested lists:

The ten most rebellious people in the Bible
The ten wisest people in the Bible
The ten most faithful women in Scripture
The ten most interesting books of the Bible
The ten Bible stories that would make the best movies
The ten best commandments
The ten most difficult times for Jesus
The ten most courageous people in Scripture
The ten worst mistakes in the Bible

■

Sweet Sixteen

Every March, college basketball fans go crazy with the NCAA tournament, in which 64 teams pair off, boiling down to 32, then the "Sweet 16," the "Elite 8," the "Final 4," and finally 2 teams playing in the final game to determine the champion. Well, why not borrow some of this hoopla to play with Scripture?

Get your family or group to come up with 16 favorite Bible verses, which you list top to bottom on a pad of paper. Select Person A as the judge for the first "game" between the top 2 verses on your list. Read the two verses aloud and have Person A select the "best" one. That verse goes into the Elite 8. For the next two verses on your list, go to Person B, and so on. Go through the list around the group. (You might ask each person why he or she chose the "winning" verse.) Boil the list down to 8, then 4, then 2, and you may want to decide the "champion" by a group vote.

Of course, it's silly to name one Bible verse as better than another, but this will be a fun game that also gets you talking about Scripture. Take every opportunity to explore the deeper meanings of the verses you read.

You could also set up competitions between Bible chapters or Bible characters. And, if you're really into it, you could set up a whole field of 64 Bible books (combining 1, 2, and 3 John).

TRAVEL GAMES

Letters to Jesus

See if each person can come up with a three-letter word that describes Jesus. Then try words of four letters, then five, then six, and so on.

What Color Is Your Paraphrase?

Read a favorite Bible verse and ask, "If this verse were a color, what color would it be?" Talk about the responses. Why that color?

Drawing Them Out

Read a favorite Bible verse or story and have the children draw it. It's amazing what they can come up with when they're forced to visualize things. Even non-story verses like John 3:16 often have visual images in them. Talk about the pictures that are drawn.

W-B-I-B-L-E News

Older children have seen enough news shows to copy the style. Read a Bible story and have the kids improvise a news report about it as correspondents for "W-B-I-B-L-E News." For instance, "Goliath is out there challenging the Israelite army again, and there seem to be no takers. But wait! There's a young man stepping out to face him. He's just a kid! How can he stand up to this giant? He's stooping down to pick up stones from the stream. What's that in his hands, a slingshot? . . ."

Section 3

family games

FAMILY GAMES

■

Bible Charades

Select Bible phrases or verses and have one person act them out for the others. The actor is not allowed to speak, but he or she can use soundalikes and syllable breakdowns for difficult words.

Team option: If you have six or more players, you may want to break into two teams and keep track of the time spent by each team. Of course, the lowest total time wins.

Here are some verses you might want to use:

"Out of the eater, something to eat; out of the strong, something sweet" (Judg. 14:14).

"He makes me lie down in green pastures, he leads me beside quiet waters" (Ps. 23:2).

"Go to the ant, you sluggard; consider its ways and be wise!" (Prov. 6:6).

"Blessed are those who hunger and thirst for righteousness, for they will be filled" (Matt. 5:6).

"I tell you, get up, take your mat and go home" (Mark 2:11).

"He has filled the hungry with good things but has sent the rich away empty" (Luke 1:53).

"I saw the Spirit come down from heaven as a dove and remain on him" (John 1:32).

"But Peter kept on knocking, and when they opened the door and saw him, they were astonished" (Acts 12:16).

"The Lord who delivered me from the paw of the lion and the paw of the bear will deliver me from the hand of this Philistine" (1 Sam. 17:37).

"Am I a dog, that you come at me with sticks?" (1 Sam. 17:43).

"It is easier for a camel to go through the eye of a needle than for a rich man to enter the kingdom of God" (Matt. 19:24).

"Sing to the Lord, for he is highly exalted. The horse and its rider he has hurled into the sea" (Exod. 15:21).

"David . . . danced before the Lord with all his might" (2 Sam. 6:14).

"You give me your shield of victory, and your right hand sustains me; you stoop down to make me great" (Ps. 18:35).

"Let your face shine on your servant; save me in your unfailing love" (Ps. 31:16).

"Hide your face from my sins and blot out all my iniquity" (Ps. 51:9).

FAMILY GAMES

Character Charades

This is like regular charades, except you act out what a Bible character did. If you get Noah, for instance, you might pretend to build an ark. This is a nice change of pace for those who know Bible characters pretty well.

Consider using the following characters:

Noah	John the Baptist	Samuel
Eve	Pontius Pilate	Nehemiah
Joseph		Mary, Jesus' mother
Moses	(More challenging)	Mary or Martha
Samson	Isaac	Lazarus
David	Rahab	Dorcas
Esther	Ruth	Rhoda
Elijah	Miriam	

Quality Quest

Take a sheet of paper for each player, write a Bible character's name at the top, and then hand out the papers, telling the players to keep their character secret. Then each player must write five words or phrases that describe this character. Creativity counts—you'll be voting later on the most enjoyable clue. (Example: "He had something in common with Dr. Doolittle." Answer: Balaam, whose donkey talked to him.)

Then have each person give his or her clues one by one, pausing so the others can guess. See who's good at guessing and who's good at cluing. And don't forget to take that vote on the most enjoyable clue.

Playing option: Make it a "Name That Tune" kind of thing, with players "bidding" on the number of clues it will take to guess the name. "I can name that character in three clues," etc.

FAMILY GAMES

Who Am I?

Choose one family member to be "It" and leave the room. The others decide (1) which Bible character that person will be, and (2) which Bible situation you will reenact. When "It" returns, the others start playing out that scene, pretending that the "It" person is the Bible character they decided on. But they cannot use the character's name—obviously, that would give it away. Continue until the player guesses who he or she is. Then repeat with other family members.

Example: (1) Moses; (2) the crossing of the Red Sea. "Look! The Egyptians are closing in on us. What are we going to do, boss? There's a sea in front of us! Can't you do something, O great leader?"

Scripture Search

Here's a challenger for a group that really knows the Bible well. Have the quizmaster open a Bible at random and read a verse. Can anyone guess what book of the Bible that verse is from? If not, the quizmaster finds another verse from the same book, and so on, until it is guessed. A correct answer earns two points, but a wrong answer loses one.

Note to quizmaster: You might give vague, nondescript verses at first, but then look for names, stories, or familiar verses.

Initials

Take the first letter of your first name and see how many Bible people, places, or objects you can think of that start with that same letter. Then try it with the first letter of your last name or the first letter of your friends' or family members' first names.

FAMILY GAMES

Mix-Up

Write the following mixed-up Bible names on index cards in large letters. When you play, hold them up and see who can be the first to unscramble them. See if the players can figure them out without using pencil and paper, but use them if you need to.

1. AIVDD

2. LUPA

3. HARBEDO

4. SHAIAI

5. SHEILA

6. HARBA

7. ESSOM

8. MYTHOIT

9. ARASH

10. TWEMTHA

11. ABCOJ

12.BURNEE

13. HARBEEK

14. TRAMAH

15. THERES

16. MONOLOS

17. SMOANS

18. ANABBARS

Of course, you can keep scrambling names on your own. Also, try scrambling names of books of the Bible or Bible places.

Ask the Pastor

Invite your pastor (and the pastor's family) over for dinner or just to sit and talk. Prepare your kids by challenging them to come up with questions about the Bible, the church, or Christian faith. (Warn the pastor to expect a grilling.)

Your pastor will probably welcome the opportunity to get to know your children better and to instruct them in the faith. And it's a great opportunity for your kids to get to know the pastor on a more informal level.

You might also try this with a Sunday school teacher or youth leader.

FAMILY GAMES

■

Sentence Builders

Here's a game for older kids. It's lots of fun and educational. Give each player a pen and paper. Everyone has to come up with one to three words or phrases in each of the following categories:

- Bible character
- Bible thing (some object mentioned in the Bible)
- Bible place
- Verb that needs an object (you do this to someone or something, like *throw, hit, call*)
- Verb that doesn't need an object (you just do it, like *run, sit, think*)
- Preposition (*in, at, across, by, of,* etc.)
- Adverb (describes a verb, often ends in *-ly*)
- Adjective (describes a person or thing)

Now, the leader chooses one of the following formats. Going around the circle, ask each person to supply the next item in the sentence.

Format A:
[Bible character] [Adverb]
[Verb needing object]
[Adjective] [Bible thing]

Format B:
[Bible character] [Adverb]
[Verb *not* needing object]
[Preposition] [Bible place]

Format C:
[Bible thing] [Adverb]
[Verb *not* needing object]
[Preposition] [Bible place]

As you construct these sentences, some will make no sense. Others will be pretty funny. And still others will come together surprisingly well. Note: The words *a, an,* and *the* are free. Put them in whenever you want. And if you want to change the tense of a verb to make it work, do it.

Example: Our word lists might look like this.

- Bible character: The Good Samaritan, Ruth, Herod
- Bible thing: Noah's ark, camel, sandal
- Bible place: Egypt, the wilderness, the Sea of Galilee
- Verb needing object: see, scold, attack
- Verb not needing object: ponder, vegetate, sneeze
- Preposition: in, over, beyond
- Adverb: happily, rudely, often
- Adjective: red, cold, gigantic

Using Format A, we might come up with: The Good Samaritan often sees the gigantic Noah's ark.

With **Format B,** it might be: Herod happily vegetated over the Sea of Galilee.

Or with **Format C:** The camel rudely sneezes in the wilderness.

Come up with your own formats or ingredients for even *more* fun.

FAMILY GAMES

How to do It

The Bible is full of good teaching, but if we only learn it in our heads, we're only going halfway. As James 1:22 says, "Do not merely listen to the word . . . Do what it says."

You can make this a family activity, tacked onto a regular Bible reading time. (If you don't already read the Bible together as a family, try starting up this new tradition, maybe once a week.)

You might call this activity "So what?" or "Just do it!" The point is to try to find ways to *live out* the Scripture that was just read. Let each child come up with a way that he or she can obey the Scripture, and then talk together about how the whole family can do so.

Example: You've just been reading in Matthew 6 about "storing your treasure in heaven." Figure out how you all can make "heavenly investments" with your money, time, and effort.

Or, you've been reading the story of David and Goliath. Ask, What sort of "Goliaths" are you going to face tomorrow? How can we develop the kind of faith and courage that David showed?

Zoo Story

Plan a family trip to the zoo. In the days preceding the trip, have the family read Bible stories that involve animals:

- Adam naming the animals (Gen. 2:19-20)
- Noah and the ark (Gen. 6–8)
- Balaam's donkey talking to him (Num. 22:21-29)
- David fighting a lion and a bear (1 Sam. 17:34-37)
- Solomon importing apes and baboons (1 Kings 10:22)
- Job hearing about behemoth (the hippo?) and other animals (Job 40:15-24; see Job 39)
- Isaiah prophesying about wolves and lions and lambs and oxen all living peacefully together (Isa. 11:6-9; 65:25)
- Daniel in the lions' den (Dan. 6)
- Jesus teaching about a camel going through the eye of a needle (Matt. 19:23-24)
- Jesus riding into Jerusalem on a donkey (Luke 19:28-44)
- Paul being bitten by a snake (Acts 28:1-6)

You could do a similar study before a trip to an aquarium or a farm.

FAMILY GAMES

Christian History

We Christians can learn a lot from each other. God has done some great things in our life, and he enjoys it when we share these stories.

Give your kids a project: to interview some older Christian and learn about his or her conversion and Christian life. Perhaps it's a grandparent they can talk to or maybe an older church member.

Help your kids develop some good questions to start with—from simple things like "How did you first become a Christian?" to something more complex, like "How did your life change in the first year after becoming a Christian?"

You can treat this as an informal project, or you can make it more formal by taking notes and writing up a report (with the permission of the interviewee, of course). You might even get school credit for a "formal" report. If that's the route you choose, show the child how to take notes when someone talks or how to use a tape recorder. If you go the informal route, be sure that your family gets an informal report about the interview.

Lost and Found

Most newspapers have a Lost and Found section in their classified pages. Clip some of these columns, and have the family read some items. Have each person make up a story about the lost (or found) object.

Who lost it?
How was it lost?
Why is it important?
Who might find it?
Would the finder want to give it back?
How would the loser feel when it was returned?

Now consider what the Bible says about lost and found things. You might center your reading on Luke 15, in which a sheep, a coin, and a son are each lost and then found.

You might close your time together by singing, "Amazing Grace": "I once was lost, but now am found. . . ."

FAMILY GAMES

Family Tree

There are some sections of the Bible that we tend to skip over. Take the beginning of Matthew, for instance—names. It's Jesus' family tree, and it seems to go on forever.

But maybe we could make more sense of passages like these if we knew more about family trees. Work with your children to develop a simple genealogy. Include brothers and sisters and parents, then uncles and aunts and grandparents, then great-uncles and great-aunts and great-grandparents—as far as you can go. (You may want to call up Grandma and Grandpa and get some earlier information from them.)

A chart like this might get you started, but try working with a bigger sheet, especially if you have a large family.

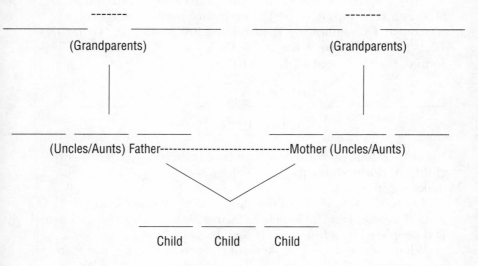

After working on this project, read through the first chapter of Matthew, and stop to talk about some recognizable characters along the way—Abraham, Rahab, Ruth, David, Hezekiah, Zerubbabel, and others.

FAMILY GAMES

Food Flight

This activity should be fun as well as tasty.

Have a family meal or snack using foods mentioned in the Bible: grapes, olives, figs, bread, grape juice, etc. Imagine yourselves as a family in Bible times.

Bake the most scrumptious bread you can, and let everyone say what they think manna tasted like.

Discuss the difficulties of preparing food without modern conveniences such as stoves and microwaves. Have you ever cooked over an open fire, perhaps on a camping trip? Talk about what that was like.

Think about how food would have been stored and preserved in ancient times, without refrigerators and canning.

Discuss how the entire family would share responsibilities in ancient times, caring for livestock, harvesting crops, etc. How can your family share the necessary food-related chores?

Consider the following food-related Bible passages: Genesis 18:1-15; Exodus 16; 1 Kings 17; Psalm 34:8-10; John 6:1-15; John 6:48-51; Romans 14:19-21.

Waiting in Line

Waiting in line, as you know, can be a difficult experience with children. But perhaps the time will go by more quickly if you make a game of it.

Try to think of times in the Bible where people might have waited in line. Did the Israelites form a line to cross the Red Sea? Did people wait in line to be healed by Jesus?

What do you think people would say to each other in those lines as they waited? What kind of clothing would they be wearing? What will be the end result of your waiting in line? (Getting into a movie, paying for groceries, etc.) What about your biblical line-waiters; what were they waiting for?

FAMILY GAMES

∎

TV Watch

For older kids, this can be a very instructive activity. Set aside a half hour or hour of TV watching as a "truth-watch" activity. When you see anything on TV that is not true, any family member can point at the TV and say "Zap!" That person then needs to explain what was untrue. If the rest of the family agrees, he or she gets a point.

For instance, a TV character might say, "If everybody's doing it, it must be OK." Zap! That's not true. Or a TV commercial might say, "You need this car." Zap! You don't.

You don't want to develop negative thinking in your children, but you do want to give them a keen sense of truth, and TV is a major source of popular falsehoods. To balance it out, you could add the "Huzzah!" factor. When something is said on TV that is especially true and good, point and say, "Huzzah!" and get another point.

∎

Flashlight Fun

This is a great activity for nighttime. Get a flashlight and turn out all the lights. One person holds the flashlight but must close his or her eyes. Another person is given a simple task (like setting the table or putting groceries away—something that requires some movement). The task-doer may not touch the flashlight but must tell the flashlight-holder (who can't see) where to shine the light. It's not as easy as it seems.

There are several biblical lessons here. One is the whole issue of teamwork. God has given each Christian a certain gift, and we need to work together to serve God (1 Cor. 12)—just as the task-doer and flashlight-holder need each other to get the job done.

Also, Jesus called his followers "the light of the world" (Matt. 5:14-16; see also John 1:4-5; Phil. 2:14-15; 1 John 1:7). Talk about what this means. How can we "shine our light" in the world around us?

You might close this activity by singing "This Little Light of Mine."

FAMILY GAMES

■

Foot Washing

In John 13, we read of Jesus washing his disciples' feet. He did this to demonstrate servanthood. His kingdom would not be about being important or "in charge." It was about humbly serving others.

Some churches practice foot washing on a regular basis, but a family can do this, too, as a simple way of following Jesus' call of servanthood. Read the text from John 13 first. Explain that, in those days and in that area, people walked in sandals along dusty roads. Their feet would get very dirty. It was the servant's job to wash the feet of guests. It was a dirty, lowly job, but someone had to do it.

Then take turns washing one another's feet in a bowl or basin of warm water. There may be some nervousness or silliness on the part of some children, but keep the focus on the example of Jesus. How does it feel to have your feet washed? How does it feel to serve someone else in this way? In the Bible account, why didn't Peter want to get his feet washed? Are there other ways that we can serve people today? How can we express our Christlike humility?

■

Sing Prayers

Many families have the habit of bedtime prayers, and many say grace before meals. But have you ever *sung* these prayers? It's something you might want to try for a change of pace.

You could select a song you know, such as "Jesus Loves Me" for a bedtime prayer, or the "Doxology" or "God Is So Good" as a mealtime prayer. Or make up your own tunes and just tell God how you feel—in song. (This is what David, the other psalmists, and a whole host of songwriters since then have done. Who knows? You may have another Isaac Watts or Fanny Crosby in your family.)

FAMILY GAMES

■

Good Investments

In Matthew 25, Jesus told of a landowner who gave money to three different servants before going away on a trip. Two of the servants invested the money, while the third just hid it in the ground.

You can try the same sort of thing with your children. Give a certain amount (over and above the normal allowance) to each child and set a six-month (or one-month or three-month) period for them to "invest" their money. Perhaps they could put up a lemonade stand during the summer and use the money to buy supplies. Perhaps they could start a savings account.

But also allow for the fact that the "return on investment" may not be financial. They may want to support a child in a needy land by sending a monthly amount. Or perhaps there are ministries in your town or state that could use financial help.

After the agreed-upon period, see what each child did with the money and what the "return" was. Read Jesus' parable again, and consider what he meant by it.

A second step might be to focus on certain talents that the children have. How are they "investing" these talents?

■

Scripture Cards

Many children enjoy collecting baseball cards or other trading cards of sports or media celebrities. Why not make your own cards of Bible characters?

You'll need some sturdy three-by-five-inch index cards and perhaps some crayons or drawing pens. Choose a Bible character—say, Simon Peter. Draw a picture of what you think he might have looked like. On the reverse side, write some facts that you know about Peter: "Disciple of Jesus . . . said Jesus was Son of God . . . denied Jesus . . . was forgiven . . . leader of early church."

You don't need to write everything right away. As you study the Bible and learn new stories, add some facts to the cards of the characters involved.

FAMILY GAMES

Prayer Scrapbook

Children can keep a prayer scrapbook containing pictures and mementos of things that they're praying for. This is a great opportunity for kids to learn about prayer, and later, as they flip through the scrapbook, they'll be reminded of how God has answered prayer.

Start with one or two simple prayer requests. The child should write down what he or she is praying for and include that in the scrapbook, along with any appropriate pictures, letters, or other documents.

Write an Epistle

Most of the New Testament is made up of letters sent by Paul and other church leaders. Try writing your own epistle to a distant relative or friend.

Read one of the shorter New Testament Epistles—2 or 3 John, or Philemon—to get a quick look at how letters were written in Bible times. Note that the writer often introduced himself, then said who the letter is written to. Often there was an expression of thanks early in the letter and praise to God. Bible letters often ended with personal information and brief prayers of praise.

You might end up with something like: "Johnny, a servant of Jesus Christ, to Grandma, a woman of great faith. I thank God whenever I think of you, for the way you taught my dad to follow Christ and the kindness you have shown to me. I want to encourage you, especially in this time of sickness, and tell you that God is faithful. He will give you the strength you need to deal with this. . . ."

Note: You may want to call the recipient before sending it, so that it won't seem too strange.

FAMILY GAMES

■

Way to Grow!

The Bible is full of references to farming and gardening. Growth is natural, both in the created world and in the Christian life. Your family could learn about spiritual and physical growth by doing some gardening together.

You could select a small spot of ground in your yard, a flower box in the window, or indoor pots. Consult a garden shop or nursery for the best plants to grow and how to care for them.

Then, after you've planted, set a time every week when the whole family can monitor the plant growth and read Bible passages about growth. Some passages might be: Psalm 1:3-4; Isaiah 5; 11:1; 53:2; Matthew 13:1-30; 1 Corinthians 3:6-9.

Ask questions such as:

How do we grow as Christians?
Plants need water and sunshine to grow. What do we need?
In what ways can we hurt the growth of plants? Can our Christian growth
  be slowed too?

Part Two

fun for one

Part Two

Europe

Section 1

word searches

WORD SEARCH

■

Water, Water Everywhere

```
F M M J O N A H G I J F R N Z
V J N E F Q E G N S D K A D W
K V O V J M M O S E S M S D U
I N P H C P V S B A O L I A W
S I E C N A I R Y W J D M V H
A T R R H T S N N J T V O I Z
A U K S P P H A O Q C F N D J
C Y I F E O T E M O Q L P N Y
N L J B J I S T B D R U E O B
E Z Q X R K K Y C A I W T A G
W I R A E R I F P G P S E H J
P S M Q W E M P Q V H T R E T
U A A N D R E W K N X B I I Y
S J A M E S V V P A U L V S X
Q T X F B A T H S H E B A S T
```

In the puzzle above, find the following 14 words or phrases, which are hidden vertically, horizontally, and diagonally.

ANDREW
BATHSHEBA
DAVID
ELISHA
ISAAC

JAMES
JOHN
JOHN THE BAPTIST
JONAH
MOSES

NOAH
PAUL
SAMARITAN WOMAN
SIMON PETER

116

WORD SEARCH

Sing a Song

```
W  J  A  M  E  S  P  R  D  E  R  X  U  D  C
L  N  Y  K  G  E  K  T  A  A  L  F  J  S  V
T  E  H  B  B  S  P  A  U  L  A  S  A  P  H
M  C  V  E  I  A  D  T  G  X  Y  L  X  Z  L
O  O  S  I  H  O  R  N  H  V  I  X  A  Z  U
U  H  O  X  T  P  G  R  T  S  H  R  N  G  I
N  P  N  F  L  E  Y  Y  E  M  Q  W  G  K  U
T  D  A  V  I  D  S  L  R  N  K  W  E  F  S
A  F  X  U  D  U  P  G  O  Y  W  D  L  G  E
I  K  S  A  E  I  M  M  F  E  J  O  S  V  S
N  H  I  Y  C  A  B  O  Z  L  P  J  M  Z  W
S  X  W  S  I  Y  R  S  I  U  Y  G  T  A  T
B  W  I  R  X  T  G  E  O  U  K  J  A  U  N
E  D  I  S  O  V  A  S  N  R  R  L  L  Y  D
J  M  X  S  O  L  O  M  O  N  H  W  I  R  X
```

In the puzzle above, find the following 14 words, which are
hidden vertically, horizontally, and diagonally.

ANGELS	DISCIPLES	MOUNTAINS
ASAPH	JAMES	PAUL
BARREN WOMAN	LEVITES	SILAS
DAUGHTER OF ZION	MIRIAM	SOLOMON
DAVID	MOSES	

WORD SEARCH

■

Fear Itself

```
K N L R S A K H X C H E T B K
U E B W M Q A Q Q S L H L A G
G O V X S J M F M J B S T D R
U B G M I A A Q X R K X J I Z
W N A L V M R J O H N B D E E
Q D E D I E Y F P N Y J V D C
A W A S H S M Q W E L E I W H
Q V H H E E A P T U W V G I A
J N A I R X G E C C A B S S R
E Q Z T O X D T M D S E S A I
A C D Z D L A E T M S P O A A
F G R F H O L R M O A E L C H
X X L P W K E T M J V R E R E
K T C U F X N C F D J S K Z D
E I U R G H E X B K O J Y W W
```

In the puzzle above, find the following 14 words, which are hidden vertically, horizontally, and diagonally.

ADAM	HEROD	MARY MAGDALENE
AHAZ	ISAAC	MOSES
DAVID	JAMES	PETER
ELIJAH	JOHN	ZECHARIAH
EVE	MARK	

WORD SEARCH

■

Shophar, So Good

```
P X P I P E L K T T
N P L X M B A R A L
T W R M L U T E M S
R C Y M B A L S B I
U T B E L L S Y O N
M S H O P H A R U G
P F L U T E H Q R I
E D X X L P A V I N
T J C H O I R S N G
T J G O N G P V E E
```

In the puzzle above, find the following 12 words, which are hidden vertically and horizontally.

BELLS	GONG	SHOPHAR
CHOIRS	HARP	SINGING
CYMBALS	LUTE	TAMBOURINE
FLUTE	PIPE	TRUMPET

WORD SEARCH

Fire Away

```
E A M U Q I Z S O L O M O N A
N A D A B A N D A B I H U Q J
A E H I O M E L I J A H D K A
J A X X S K S P V J T I U D M
E Q R D J R G H P H O E W C E
Z F D O I R A Y A G C D I T S
E R G H N M X E E D A K O I A
B Y W W V O L N L K R C G J N
E S F F N S D O I I J A F R D
L G V U L E F Q T L T G C N J
S K W P B S Q D H O C E M H O
B N W A C S A T A N W V S S H
B A L D I J O S H U A L J P N
Y F Q Q V H X M U K N X B W M
J M E S H A C H K J L E A E T
```

In the puzzle above, find the following 14 words, which are hidden vertically, horizontally, and diagonally.

AARON	JEZEBEL	NADAB AND ABIHU
ABEDNEGO	JOSHUA	SATAN
ELIJAH	LOT	SHADRACH
ISRAELITES	MESHACH	SOLOMON
JAMES AND JOHN	MOSES	

WORD SEARCH

Animal Tales

```
B J R N F W X I D A V I D R W
Y E F D V C O B H O S Z A N X
M Y T H U H N A S K T Z L W J
D O T H W U O D A J Z Q S G O
A H L X L N R V B E J E K B N
N E N U R E M C N A L A A Z A
I C A U H X H D B B L J X W H
E S R P M S A E A N J A V K Z
L Y E P J H A R M U P K A R W
O H N H C H A M V S Z F T M J
S Z L U U P A U S T T Q Z X J
B G B J H N V W G O H A M Y O
P E X N Q A D A M A N E B Z P
N J O B M N M O H D H W J L C
K A A R O N M N J W W M E C E
```

In the puzzle above, find the following 14 words, which are hidden vertically, horizontally, and diagonally.

AARON	DAVID	PARABLES
ADAM	JOB	SAMSON
BALAAM	JONAH	SAUL
BETHLEHEM STABLE	NEBUCHADNEZZAR	SHEPHERDS
DANIEL	NOAH	

WORD SEARCH

Hide and Seek

```
B N Q O U V D O O T Y I W P E
N Y H E O G O D S F A C E E Z
P T U T V N F O K O D K J O R
T B U Q P X E A S L O V E P T
L C A G D T N T U P C E L L Q
A H P B O B R J A L I U I E T
S G R X Y D G E O L T E Z S B
A N O T Q M S Z A A E S S F X
J U P G C A O W G S S N O A W
G A H F R O D S O E U H T C E
U E E A E Z P T E R T R T E L
V H T K O D J J R S D T E S I
U Q S D K G Y P D N B E L S J
J A H U U H S A U L M S G Q A
F R A N A G W I S D O M D M H
```

In the puzzle above, find the following 14 words, which are hidden vertically, horizontally, and diagonally.

BABY MOSES	JOASH	SAUL
ELIJAH	LOVE	SPIES
FAULTS	ONE TALENT	TREASURES
GOD'S FACE	PEOPLE'S FACES	WISDOM
GOD'S WORD	PROPHETS	

WORD SEARCH

Pot of Gold

```
H  J  E  S  H  R  A  P  P  L  E  S  Z  S  B
V  N  E  O  F  E  P  E  C  R  O  W  N  G  R
N  T  S  L  E  P  A  V  P  I  W  O  H  G  E
U  R  L  O  U  A  N  D  P  C  I  P  V  R  A
B  U  Z  M  T  L  R  V  O  L  I  E  C  U  S
G  M  C  O  H  K  W  R  S  F  V  O  T  F  T
O  P  C  N  E  R  H  L  I  S  I  I  S  V  P
L  E  Z  S  S  U  E  K  O  N  O  M  O  Q  L
D  T  C  W  U  I  A  F  J  K  G  R  A  Q  A
E  S  Y  E  N  A  T  B  X  K  R  S  O  G  T
N  G  X  A  Y  I  W  Z  G  E  V  C  P  P  E
C  C  D  L  T  Z  N  X  C  H  A  I  N  S  N
A  Z  I  T  D  A  V  I  D  S  H  A  R  P  V
L  I  N  H  K  T  L  W  O  U  X  V  B  J  Q
F  U  W  I  S  E  M  E  N  S  G  I  F  T  V
```

In the puzzle above, find the following 14 words, which are hidden vertically, horizontally, and diagonally.

APPLES	DAVID'S HARP	THE SUN
BREASTPLATE	EARRINGS	TRUMPETS
CHAINS	GOLDEN CALF	WHEAT
CROWN	HEAD OF IMAGE	WISE MEN'S GIFT
DANIEL'S LIONS	SOLOMON'S WEALTH	

WORD SEARCH

Up a Tree

```
R T Q T L I L B O E H B E D P
S H F E A N B Q F I G E S S L
Y E I B L G B I I O R U S M A
C C G F F Y L S F T S E O Q N
A R X E H F P I N E R O K X T
M O R Q O N W E J P D V G R E
O S D E R G D Y Y S E E K E D
R S E A M D B C M T L E V F B
E R D J I D O O Y T N I U E Y
T E O B E X L V R P L F K K R
C J R S M A E Y B O E T A M I
A O R I S J M L H M U Q L I V
F U Z B A L Z B I N Y A E Y E
C R A F Q P D U D W P Y L K R
S T U M P O F J E S S E Q N S
```

In the puzzle above, find the following 14 words, which are hidden vertically, horizontally, and diagonally.

ABSALOM'S DOOM	FORBIDDEN TREE	STUMP OF JESSE
CEDAR	MYRTLE	SYCAMORE
CURSED BY JESUS	OLIVE	THE CROSS
CYPRESS	PALM	TREE OF LIFE
FIG	PLANTED BY RIVERS	

WORD SEARCH

■

Acquainted with Angels

```
L  L  G  K  N  G  A  B  R  I  E  L  F  M  C
F  V  I  A  B  H  J  L  B  M  N  I  S  I  U
J  Y  Q  A  R  V  A  M  F  O  A  D  V  C  B
C  H  Z  Z  S  D  O  G  E  L  R  Z  K  H  A
R  Y  O  X  Q  T  E  D  A  E  S  M  F  A  L
Z  Y  V  D  S  C  I  N  H  R  N  A  Y  E  A
K  N  L  U  R  G  T  P  O  A  L  R  M  L  A
Q  V  S  T  H  P  E  Z  J  F  S  Y  P  K  M
A  E  L  M  L  H  N  G  C  G  E  V  C  B  S
J  J  L  N  S  M  A  N  O  A  H  D  I  V  D
C  Z  R  I  J  T  H  K  D  I  T  Z  E  T  O
M  J  A  C  O  B  S  D  R  E  A  M  A  N  N
P  E  T  E  R  I  N  P  R  I  S  O  N  L  K
K  Y  M  O  S  E  S  P  Y  R  T  G  T  Y  E
V  F  D  Z  E  C  H  A  R  I  A  H  O  Z  Y
```

In the puzzle above, find the following 14 words, which are hidden vertically, horizontally, and diagonally.

BALAAM'S DONKEY	JACOB'S DREAM	MOSES
GABRIEL	JESUS' TOMB	PETER IN PRISON
GARDEN OF EDEN	MANOAH	SHEPHERDS
GIDEON	MARY	ZECHARIAH
HAGAR	MICHAEL	

WORD SEARCH

■

Bodies of Water

```
O E X G R E A T S E A B W J N
E C U C C K I D R O N E X A K
A E M P Z Z H C D Z M A E B E
S J G I H O N S P R I N G B B
E A P O F R A K F U A N A O A
A C G X X Q A R E R I I P K R
O O D N C O X T R D A L X R R
F B W T C B M E E E E E V I I
G S Y W C L T L S S W X B V V
A W N E S I A D R U R D H E E
L E C S D Q E Q P S W I T R R
I L W E M R Z S A C D Z V L A
L L M P H D E A D S E A F E Z
E E N G E D I S P R I N G S R
E K F A J O R D A N H M E D Q
```

In the puzzle above, find the following 14 words, which are hidden vertically, horizontally, and diagonally.

DEAD SEA	JABBOK RIVER	MEDITERRANEAN
ENGEDI SPRINGS	JACOB'S WELL	NILE
EUPHRATES RIVER	JORDAN	RED SEA
GIHON SPRING	KEBAR RIVER	SEA OF GALILEE
GREAT SEA	KIDRON	

WORD SEARCH

Kings

```
Z O B A M A Z H A I A K E Z E H Z H
P T A H P A H S O H E J H N L F A Z
K F Y A H M E X E X Q H O U Z I D N
E J P N V C D T N B I R A N K O C E
S O V X E A K O E A E S E E R R V B
O A S B I B M A I H D B Z R A L W U
L S J V M O U K Y A B E E Z K P J C
O H I R L Y E C V U H H E A J K O H
M D P S U Z D I C A Z M R G S M T A
O N X X Z O D H I H D X H H A A H D
N R H E R I A K Z A A E S O B Y A N
R W H E I D E W H S S D B A S V M E
Y Y H V N Z H C Q S O O N O W N Q Z
G M A E Z M U A A U H L L E W L L Z
X D Z E T B F N I E N O O J Z V B A
Y E H S E G A Q R S N E G M A R N R
R Z S N D M K D W O O K V S I V J Z
I B X D Q D J G M P A J Y L W N I E
```

In the puzzle above, find the following 14 words, which are hidden vertically, horizontally, diagonally, and backwards.

AHAB	JEHOSHAPHAT	NEBUCHADNEZZAR
ASA	JOASH	REHOBOAM
DAVID	JOSIAH	SAUL
HEROD	JOTHAM	SOLOMON
HEZEKIAH	MANASSEH	

127

WORD SEARCH

■

Apostles

In the puzzle above, find the following 12 words, which are hidden vertically, horizontally, diagonally, and backwards.

ANDREW	JOHN	PHILIP
BARTHOLOMEW	JUDAS ISCARIOT	SIMON PETER
JAMES SON OF ALPHAEUS	JUDAS NOT ISCARIOT	SIMON THE ZEALOT
JAMES SON OF ZEBEDEE	MATTHEW	THOMAS

WORD SEARCH

People Jesus Knew

```
N I C O D E M U S F E E D E B E Z R
M U Y N U T B D E A N S J U R J A E
B A M A R T H A L L U O R Z O V Z T
J T R K R E E A S E S E W E C S Q A
A O Q Y C L Z Y A E P L T Q I N N L
X O H Z M A R M P E P A S M Q A Z P
Z W F N R A I H L D L M O Q M R M I
H V C U T T G E Z I O N H O F S A T
E T S A R H H D P Z T R W U S U R T
R L O A I T E S A H E N E U X R A N
O B B W N A U B H L A B E H M A T O
B K K O J I P L A T E A D Y F L H P
X A M E T M E H I P H N R E A A A Z
Z I H N C O E R A C T A E A B Z M B
S Q O P P G A A C S R I K G B E I Y
N P E A R M K A K M Y C S I W G W R
I R R X A R Z Q Z N W U G T Y D G A
E D K S S S U E H C A Z Z E F Q Q M
```

In the puzzle above, find the following 14 words, which are hidden vertically, horizontally, diagonally, and backwards.

BARTIMAEUS	LAZARUS	PONTIUS PILATE
CAIAPHAS	MARTHA	SAMARITAN WOMAN
HEROD	MARY	SIMON THE LEPER
JOHN THE BAPTIST	MARY MAGDALENE	ZACCHAEUS
JOSEPH	NICODEMUS	

WORD SEARCH

Women of the Bible

```
V M J E Z E B E L G X M T A K
E A N W B V L J J I L D L A D
S R S G L T V W S E S L T L I
T Y A R Y S D Y T A I A E F X
H X B Q E R U T H C J H R X I
E O A M I B Y H S A C C P A J
R I T I F O E I N A Y J V Y H
W C H R E L R K R W S W H B G
D L S I T P D N A A W A T O E
M H H A I J I K I H R H D H Z
A A E M D S Z D Y O A G I A K
R G B F E M O I B D A R E N S
T A A C R R T E L A F V Q N W
H R Q J E X D U I H E V M A V
A O Q H D J H L E A H O L H U
```

In the puzzle above, find the following 18 words, which are hidden vertically, horizontally, and diagonally.

BATHSHEBA	HERODIAS	MIRIAM
DEBORAH	HULDAH	PRISCILLA
ESTHER	JEZEBEL	RACHEL
EVE	LEAH	REBEKAH
HAGAR	MARTHA	RUTH
HANNAH	MARY	SARAH

WORD SEARCH

Books of the New Testament

```
W C O L O S S I A N S Y R U R
T F Y G E U T B W Y J O H N E
I T I M P H I L E M O N G V V
T W A R V E S M G R M H S O E
U J T L S W P S K E E N S W L
S C Q K E T T H A Q A C L R A
L D R R A C T J E I H T L Q T
T A B R A X F I P S G Q R W I
M E I Y N V L P M O I Y C W O
H J Z W X W I Y R O N A E R N
G J U D E L U K E T T H N M U
W X T G I U K C Z U T H E S S
N U Z H R R K D R T C I Y Q G
P I P K X R Q N A W U G D P S
Q R O M A N S M W Y F Q Q V A
```

In the puzzle above, find the following 16 words, which are hidden vertically, horizontally, and diagonally.

ACTS	JOHN	PHILIPPIANS
COLOSSIANS	JUDE	REVELATION
EPHESIANS	LUKE	ROMANS
FIRST TIMOTHY	MARK	TITUS
HEBREWS	MATTHEW	
JAMES	PHILEMON	

WORD SEARCH

Beasts and Birds

```
E Q D O C D T E G K F V Z A Z
B N Q O U J O S T R I C H E S
Q P X Z N P H A W K S N J V D
Z R I J E K F T I K G O A T S
S R P E H N E R A A O S Y M W
M W H H Q Z D Y O M Z F C L D
O S I G O L O O S G M S B I M
N R D N B R G P Q T S W G K E
U S S R E U S M C A M E L S S
Q T D M B P P E A C O C K S N
P X O U R T P B S Q F L C W A
G C V L X E J B L I O N S A K
U U E E I W H A L E S M S G E
Q G S S S Q U A I L B H B A S
J S Q C U Z C A F O X E S G O
```

In the puzzle above, find the following 18 words, which are hidden vertically, horizontally, and diagonally.

CAMELS	GOATS	PEACOCKS
DOGS	HAWKS	QUAIL
DONKEYS	HORSES	SHEEP
DOVES	LIONS	SNAKES
FOXES	MULES	SWINE
FROGS	OSTRICHES	WHALES

WORD SEARCH

Bible Places

```
H A R A R A T L Q I I B B P N
T O M N O D B E T H L E H E M
A O R O X N Z E G Y P T D C I
J G V E U P O L C U S E E O J
E E W Z B N B E C A F I R R E
R T Q I A R T C C O N E O I R
U H H O T L H O N J S A M N I
S S Y N G A E E F I W Z E T C
A E X B D W D X D O L J J H H
L M I U L R D A A A L E T L O
E A J G A Z R H J N K I E G S
M N H G W A O M R B D A V W S
Z E E V P V P I W H R R N E U
L U N P E R S I A S P C I W S
U R A G R C O G I L E A D A R
```

In the puzzle above, find the following 20 words, which are hidden vertically, horizontally, and diagonally.

ALEXANDRIA	GETHSEMANE	MOUNT OF OLIVES
ARARAT	GILEAD	NOD
BETHLEHEM	HOREB	PARADISE
CANA	ISRAEL	PERSIA
CORINTH	JERICHO	ROME
EGYPT	JERUSALEM	ZION
GARDEN OF EDEN	JUDAH	

WORD SEARCH

What's for Dinner?

```
M R C I C V J U T B E H Y B H
A A P P L E S C M T P C I R F
O O L I V E S A A M M Y V E F
H F D B H P L N X I A B G A I
S I P O T T A G E P N E F D S
V G F C O R N I M H N X B N H
B S B L G A W I L P A E I H L
K S U E V G L R E L I S A O R
S C M N Q R T M A Y I L P N P
B O C T P A W T O A A O O E Y
P N Z I I P V H R N I C O Y L
U M X L P E U X E V D U B W D
H I M S Y S W K L A C S F O S
N D B B A D V Y C K T T K J S
M M I L K O K W L A Z S Q K V
```

In the puzzle above, find the following 18 words, which are hidden vertically, horizontally, and diagonally.

ALMONDS	GRAPES	MILK
APPLES	HONEY	OLIVES
BREAD	LAMB	POMEGRANATE
CORN	LENTILS	POTTAGE
FIGS	LOCUSTS	RAISINS
FISH	MANNA	WHEAT

WORD SEARCH

Books of the Old Testament

```
K G Y P Q P S A L M S A P R Y D O N
U O H V G Y M O N O R E T U E D E F
G B O J W F S L E I K E Z E Y H A N
R U T H M A G N D M K W H T E P N T
D H B J S A Y U G N T S E M U J K S
I A A K N G L N H O R S I M B G R G
S I N F I T N A O X S A A S A E Q S
A S W I W E I O C M H F N M B G H O
M I W S E D I Q S H O O O M E M E M
U X V W A L H V X F I R U N E U D A
E U B B N C N B S T O N E F G M L A
L J O Z L G I Z A R S G T T G O M J
I S A I A H S T E H E G N K U V S N
A U H S O J N S S E A B N O V D T X
Z I P T U E Y K I I K N M I S W Y X
N D M R M L B Z Z Y V I O M K B T X
A I W A S I S E N E G L E J U I V D
Y A L E V I T I C U S W E L I Z I X
```

In the puzzle above, find the following 20 words, which are hidden vertically, horizontally, diagonally, and backwards.

AMOS	JOB	NUMBERS
DANIEL	JONAH	OBADIAH
DEUTERONOMY	JOSHUA	PSALMS
EZEKIEL	LAMENTATIONS	RUTH
GENESIS	LEVITICUS	I SAMUEL
ISAIAH	MALACHI	SONG OF SONGS
II KINGS	NEHEMIAH	

WORD SEARCH

Genesis

```
M C H D T E W D G K S F T U S S R U
E M O M V Q A T C J P I D O B L G H
L D A E P G E T A S A J M O L D O H
C H R A C H E L B I J P C E E L U A
H C A I N Q S I E I S A H P O A P K
I D H A N I D H L H J A N E S N B E
Z L P B H C E L E M I B A E T N R B
E R A G A H H W R M C I W C U H E E
D R B Z A K A A C W Y H S X C L U R
E L W P M A H A R B A J X H C N B Z
K E L T A C L N R L O A H H M U E E
D I I C A S I X E S S S X A W A N B
Z Z R S O M B S E E S H H D R H E U
U N S L A V U P T X Y E A U U A L L
G I M J E H H H V K N R E J C A S U
V P N A T V A E N O C H L D B V Q N
X E C E D U I T A N R A M A T G U F
B L M I L A T H P A N S N N J S L B
```

Somehow we crammed 42 names from Genesis into this puzzle. For extra credit, explain who each of these people is!

ABEL	HAGAR	METHUSELAH
ABIMELECH	HAM	NAPHTALI
ABRAHAM	ISAAC	NOAH
ADAM	ISHMAEL	PHARAOH
ASHER	ISSACHAR	RACHEL
BENJAMIN	JACOB	REBEKAH
BILHAH	JAPHETH	REUBEN
CAIN	JOSEPH	SARAH
DAN	JUDAH	SETH
DINAH	LABAN	SHEM
ENOCH	LEAH	SIMEON
ESAU	LEVI	TAMAR
EVE	LOT	ZEBULUN
GAD	MELCHIZEDEK	ZILPAH

WORD SEARCH

Numbers

```
P O W E R F U L S K H X K C G Z X D
D N E T A E B S T G N G R N O E E P
O F O O T E E A R A N U I S C N H A
N O W O S N E E R N S T D N N T T F
K R G R N F C R E H S E I I Q P A R
E A U O E N O V I U S R S Q E F P E
Y C I D U W E N R U P N F T O R W W
F L H O P S G C F O A X H O Z B O A
Z E N A D T Z E E R S O L P K L R R
E E T D X E R R R G R U O L W E R D
D N V R X J N O E A N W M J Z S R Z
S B A O M C W N B T E H F M S S A R
E X O W M P U C N R P B S E O H N E
C F E S A O N R F I A E N U E N Z W
N Q S T A R U A E L S O C M R X I O
I Q H U L Q L T A S I Z O S U C D R
R L K V A P T K H L A N G E L F X D
P R O E B E S R U C A L T A R S D R
```

Find the following words referring to the life of Balaam in the puzzle on the opposite page.

ALTARS
ANGEL
BALAAM
BALAK
BEATEN
BEOR
BLESS
CRUSHING
CURSE
DEFEAT

DENOUNCE
DONKEY
FEE
FOOL
FOOT
LIONESS
MOAB
MOUTH
NARROW PATH
ORACLE

POWERFUL
PRINCES
REFUSED
REWARD
SCEPTER
SEVEN
SINNED
STAR
SUMMON
SWORD

WORD SEARCH

Ruth

```
K G B K K M S S E N I M A F U V H R
S I E I A L T E V I T A L E R A I A
A R N E T A M S S S N C Q E P R W W
W T L S R T N E E S R A E R E A A A
Z G W A M O E V H E E M O M F L A S
Z S M A I A R R T E D N E M N T L H
S P A L L R N T W E L D T I I S N C
Q D I N A N T R R N E H R I E E I E
J K L H D I I N E R O E T M W V R L
B N Y E B L A R N D H L U E L R E E
A A W X I M K A T T E F H A B A H M
R E I V S F M R O S R E D A V H T I
L L F N W N E M W E I N M E M J O L
E G I H I T Z I P I A S O E B B M E
Y K E K U L W A H S F D A Q R O D J
Y A Z R H U S B A N D E B W I N G S
T Z N S G I W A L N I R E T S I S G
Y E L R R A B Z S E V A E H S P O Z
```

Find these key words from the book of Ruth in the puzzle on the opposite page.

BARLEY	KINSMAN-REDEEMER	RETURN
BETHLEHEM	MAHLON	SANDAL
BITTER	MARA	SHAWL
ELIMELECH	MOAB	SHEAVES
FAMINE	MOTHER-IN-LAW	SISTER-IN-LAW
FIELDS	NAOMI	WASH
GLEAN	OBED	WHEAT
HARVEST	ORPAH	WIFE
HUSBAND	PERFUME	WINGS
KILION	RELATIVE	WITNESSES

WORD SEARCH

Elijah & Elisha (1 & 2 Kings)

```
D E R M A L E M R A C N U O M Z F H
E R A C D Z A R E P A T H N E A I E
M U V M B O H Q W C W H I S P E R M
U O E D Y T U H N I L T W L D I E D
S L N Z I F I B E A R O E I F L O S
N F S R E R L N L O A E A O N U B E
O E E E L R I E P P R M T K B D R Y
C K R W A M I E M T O O A L S C O E
C A I I A R L F M A I R E N H O O C
V N R F F B T O F R R P T T W N N I
D D J A U F O H A O O A A I I N T F
U I U O M R O H Q R T H C A O S R I
H T D O B E C T T U P O T T C N E R
S A L T L I A I I E A P I L N J E C
K O O R B C O N R R A K I R A U F A
W O D I W N O A S C A N E Y A A O S
D A E H X A Z B A L D H E A D H B M
M O U N T C A R M E L Q C P O T C V
```

Find the words referring to the lives of Elijah and Elisha in the puzzle on the opposite page.

ARAMEANS
AX HEAD
BAAL
BALD HEAD
BROOK
BROOM TREE
CAPTAIN
CHARIOT OF FIRE
CLOAK
CLOUD

CONSUMED
DOUBLE PORTION
EARTHQUAKE
EYES
FAMINE
FIRE
FLOUR
KERITH
MOUNT CARMEL
NAAMAN

OIL
POT
RAVENS
SACRIFICE
SALT
SON
WHIRLWIND
WHISPER
WIDOW
WIND
ZAREPHATH

WORD SEARCH

■

Life of David (1 Chronicles)

```
N E K N L R P H I L I S T I N E S Z
J E R U S A L E M M M A K L Q Z M C
M O L A S B A S H I P A F I I A O J
N S S Z Z I K L A G M W R O R B N O
O G E E O E K B Y H I N N I N I O A
N Z F T C D I F H Y G H A V H A L B
M I D N I G A I E T H T R T B T O S
A C J I A N L Z B N T A A S H H S I
M L I I V H O U R E Y G U O J A Z N
J A L B B A T M O M M A N L K R N G
E G Z A E A D A M Y E R A O O Y Q E
B O A T T B S F N A N M H M D I U R
U T B H H I H E O O T A O O A J Z S
S A S S L G E E T Y J T J N Z B Z A
I M A H E A U N B I T X L U A S A B
T A L E H L M S Z R V I Q Z S U H H
E R O B E E B A W G O E C E Q A N A
S Y N A M Z B O A J E N L H P A S A
```

Find the words referring to people and places in the life of David in the puzzle on the opposite page.

ABIATHAR
ABIGAIL
ABSALOM
AMMONITES
AMNON
ARAUNAH
ASAPH
BATHSHEBA
BETHLEHEM
CITY OF DAVID

GATH
HEBRON
HIRAM
JEBUSITES
JERUSALEM
JOAB
JONATHAN
LEVITES
MIGHTY MEN
NATHAN

PHILISTINES
SAUL
SINGERS
SOLOMON
TAMAR
UZZAH
ZADOK
ZIKLAG
ZION

WORD SEARCH

Job

```
X S O C E S P F S S E L E M A L B I
S W R S R E T H G U A D G S E R O S
D U H I L E E E S O L E S S R D E G
A Y C D O N K E Y S F D T A N I N R
D Z U H P I L E R Q Y S H E T M A O
L Y A W A N E K A T A P X R E T K A
I E E Z O P H A D E O Q A X V Q E M
B K S G D R H G F Z Z P O X R B D I
W N C H D S Z E E V G Y V E P P D N
P O O T U E Z N L N X B H N L E Z G
S D N I D N H G I I L O B G I I I G
A G S S E D N D N E P I O F I C H N
B N I L P N I E S I L H I X U R L Y
E I D E A A I S D D Z R A R E W P O
A Z E G R U E K A E U A S Z X N V U
N A R N C D A R S P V E S L E M A C
S R E A S J X J U P R I G H T D E J
U G D L R E G N I F A H L Y B L P J
```

Find the words referring to the story of Job in the puzzle on the opposite page.

ANGELS	ELIPHAZ	SABEANS
BILDAD	FEASTS	SCRAPED
BLAMELESS	FINGER	SHUNNED EVIL
BLESSED	GRAZING	SKIN
CAMELS	HEDGE	SOLES
CONSIDERED	NAKED	SORES
CURSE	OXEN	TAKEN AWAY
DAUGHTERS	PURIFIED	UPRIGHT
DONKEYS	RAIDING PARTIES	ZOPHAR
ELIHU	ROAMING	

WORD SEARCH

Proverbs 31

```
Y L S U O R O G I V B L E S S E D F
I F G N O I T C U R T S N I H E E A
C E N I R S Y L J M S M C W U C H L
D A I A X T C I O E U R O O S O T X
O R D L M R E N Z R P A N O B N O F
O S A A R O L E F C P H S L A F L L
G T R F U N P N E H L C I S N I C A
B H T I B G R G A A I E D U D D P X
R E B N I Z U A R N U A E P S E R D
H L O E E G P R N T E G R P L N O I
O O P L S Q B M I S S E S L L C F G
U R E I E Q U E N H P R W I E E I N
S D N N Y D Y N G I I Q I E S E T I
E D S E S L S T S P N X Y S L S A T
H X W N Z E I S K S D O R B W H B Y
O D E L E I F M Z G L G O O U O L Q
L D L I E F X R A N E N N Z H V E D
D C I T Y G A T E F V S E H S A S M
```

Proverbs 31 is a paean to the "good woman." At first glance that may rankle some modern thinkers, but notice how modern the description is. This is an enterprising businesswoman as well as an efficient homemaker and devoted wife and mother—a modern woman if ever there was one. The high expectations indicate it was written either by a man (King Lemuel, verse 1), or by a "Type A" woman (his mother?).

BLESSED
BUYS
CHARM
CITY GATE
CLOTHED
CONFIDENCE
CONSIDERS
DIGNITY
EAGER
EARNINGS
FAMILY
FEARS THE LORD

FIELD
FINE LINEN
FLAX
GOOD
HOUSEHOLD
HUSBAND
INSTRUCTION
LINEN GARMENTS
MERCHANT SHIPS
NOBLE
OPENS
PROFITABLE

PURPLE
RUBIES
SASHES
SELLS
SNOWS
SPINDLE
STRONG
SUPPLIES
TRADING
VIGOROUSLY
WOOL

WORD SEARCH

■

Jonah

```
D E R E H T I W R Y O J J O P P A T
E D A H S E R C E D A X G R Y A N G
T A R S H I S H N S O W X M T O R S
K R W W Z N N I H C A L A M I T Y W
A D O F N D W Y F M D L X N C L E A
R N R G I T I H Y I N E V B A S A L
E A M X S E G S O F Q B R A R R N L
L L C A Q O R V T S U W E O T D S O
E Y E A R H E C S E O O L E T I T W
N R T I P R E E E H S I E E G Y O V
T D G C B T R B T A A S S R N K R N
S H B O I T A O R S N E T C I W M G
T D A Y S N L I S E V G S E F K Z R
U R M I J C M C N A W I E D L I K E
D I D Q K S X D W O R N T R U N I N
T I P C G R E A T F I S H P G G N I
B J A F E D A N S Y X J K U N J Q V
L S R O L I A Z A N G R Y S E B I O
```

You will notice the word *whale* does not appear here. A puzzle-maker's oversight? Nope. The text says a "great fish" that swallowed Jonah. Can you imagine the "fish story" that creature told his buddies? ("He was this big . . . but I threw him back.")

ANGRY
CALAMITY
CAPTAIN
CITY
DECREE
DISTRESS
DRY LAND
EAST WIND
ENGULFING
GREAT FISH

HEBREW
JOPPA
KING
OVERBOARD
PIT
RAN AWAY
RELENT
RIGHT
SACKCLOTH
SAILORS

SALVATION
SHADE
STORM
SWALLOW
TARSHISH
VINE
WAVES
WITHERED
WORM

WORD SEARACH

Habakkuk

```
I R E G N I L T G N Q E W I N E H I
G N O T O X N D I K D D R I N K V M
A E C H Z E F A X T R T A K W E I A
L Y C E R T G I O V E N G J A R O G
L E E I N T R L S H A E E I B U L E
O D S C S S E A S K D L N S B T E W
P X O U C R E I M U E I O N D L N A
S R J A A O F Y K B D S T A E U C T
V N S T R A P M A R L H S I S V E E
U D E H O R D E S D B E H N P P X R
O E I B E N Q T S Y G S D O A L T S
C L P E R E G N A L E Z F L L E E T
H P G N I T S A L R E V E Y L O G E
E M K R O W D O O W J T W B O P A L
Z A S P M A R A Q H C E Z A C A R B
V R K P P T E N G A R D O B R R D A
C T G J E T I R W Y R A M B S D Z T
Z F F N P Q E L U C I D I R M S Y G
```

Good writing uses crisp words. We see lots of those in these prophetic books. If you're puzzling over vague business memos, product instructions that are hard to follow, or journals that require a doctorate just to read the table of contents—enjoy the crisp diction of Habakkuk, Haggai, Malachi, and the others. They talk about ordinary folks such as launderers and refiners, common objects such as paneling and woodwork, and creatures such as calves and leopards. Their verbs are strong and visual (**gallop, trample, shake, leap**). You can sink your teeth into writing like this. So, after you finish these puzzles, why not munch on a chapter or two? And "Merry Crispness!"

BABYLONIANS	IMAGE	TABLETS
COLLAPSED	INCENSE	TOLERATE
DRAGNET	LEOPARDS	TRAMPLED
DREADED	LINGER	UNJUST GAIN
DRINK	RAGE	VIOLENCE
ECHO	RAMPARTS	VULTURE
EVERLASTING	RAMPS	WATERS
FISH	RIDICULE	WINE
GALLOPS	SILENT	WOODWORK
HORDES	STONE	WRITE

WORD SEARCH

Malachi

```
D A B O C A J N E D R U B I H S L Q
R C Z O P F P R E G N E S S E M S W
O E R I F S R E N I F E R L S R D H
L L S L A K C A J W M L A E N Z E C
E C R O P A O S A G V U V B I Q I O
H S O T F P C S J F N L Y E O Q R N
T A N O Q F T X G D A W L N L U A T
S H O H U E E N E C Y B F E D N E E
I D H P L Y I R L S A Y A N E A W M
T K U A B L E N I T E P E K U N R P
A N N A A R L R S N Z T H K E S E T
E D S E S L Q D D C G E T K N F T C
R E H T D E R T W E C S O I U G U K
G L E I R O C U S R F R S R N R R U
R C M T L A Q H O T B I N C P G N P
O A X H S T E V E G S A L H W V M G
B R R E M H I H O A C T L E L E E S
W O C S Q D A Q C E T L Y S D R O X
```

Locate these keywords found in the book of Malachi in the puzzle on the oppoite page.

BROKEN	HEALING	ORACLE
BURDEN	HEARTS	REFINER'S FIRE
CALVES	HONORS	RETURN
CHEAT	JACKALS	ROB
CONTEMPT	JACOB	SETTING
DEFILED	LAUNDERERS	SOAP
DIVORCE	LEAP	SUN
ESAU	LORD'S TABLE	TITHES
FURNACE	MESSENGER	WASTELAND
GREAT IS THE LORD	OFFERINGS	WEARIED

WORD SEARCH

Matthew

```
R S W Z Y D M M X W Y M M D O T H P
F A M J S W R T H E E A I F E G Z V
Z B A O C U C E L D E G L G B B C R
D B K Q G Y W M E D Q I L S A A T U
E A E G D U J P U I V R S L P Y A M
R R D H D D U T N N H U T O T S L O
U A I O A O H E A G E E O O I R E R
G B S S I S D D M B R L N F Z O N S
I U C A L A R G M A O D E D E T T O
F M I N Y B A S I N D E B N T C S F
S K P N B B Y O S Q I E L I F E A W
N R L A R A E W T U A N E L R L E A
A O E V E T N E I E S A S B E L Y R
R O S C A H I R A T X F S H E O F S
T S Q B D O V R P V W O E E L C O P
U T C E N T U R I O N E D Z Y X W L
T E V F C R U M B S P Y M H W A B B
A R D V N O T T U L G E S V L T R R
```

There are 28 words in this puzzle and 28 chapters in Matthew. Guess what? Each of these is a keyword of one of Matthew's chapters. As an extra game, figure out which word applies to which chapter.

BAPTIZE	HERODIAS	SOWER
BARABBAS	HOSANNA	TALENTS
BLESSED	IMMANUEL	TAX COLLECTORS
BLIND FOOLS	JUDGE	TEMPTED
CENTURION	MAGI	TRANSFIGURED
CRUMBS	MAKE DISCIPLES	VINEYARD
DAILY BREAD	MILLSTONE	WEDDING BANQUET
EYE OF A NEEDLE	ROOSTER	YEAST
FREELY	RUMORS OF WARS	
GLUTTON	SABBATH	

WORD SEARCH

John

```
L D E T P H Y Z Y F I R O L G J W Y
W R N D I S Z T M A L K Y P Y R E R
T E I F E L Y E L O O P B K D I L E
U H W A M F R N L R Z H R L N F L S
R P P T U B A S I N D E V F A P H U
L E G H F W O R D W A B A C S E A R
E H H E R E T E P N O M I S U E L R
C S W R E D C L M N O K I G O H I E
O D W O P E A S J I T D N R H S T C
U O S F N S V U B A Z R O E T Y T T
R O P L I X I K S G P K B E E M L I
T G I I C Y N C S A I I B K V D E O
Y W T E O G E A E N L D A S I E W N
A P Y S D L Y H L R A D R A F E H J
R B M E E K N T M O T L Q L T F I W
D X C W M O L R A B E A B R U E L I
D S A F U G F A E S U H C L A M E H
A Y D H S P D M S C K F H C P Q F E
```

We'll make this even more difficult for you. There are 26 words in this puzzle, one for each of the 21 chapters of John plus 5 others that have something in common. If you can, figure out which word goes with each chapter and which 5 words are special.

BASIN
BORN AGAIN
COURTYARD
FATHER OF LIES
FEED MY SHEEP
FIVE THOUSAND
GLORIFY
GOOD SHEPHERD
GREEKS

LITTLE WHILE
MALCHUS
MARTHA
NICODEMUS
PERFUME
PILATE
POOL
RABBONI
RESURRECTION

SEAMLESS
SIMON PETER
SPIT
VINE
WAY
WELL
WINE
WORD

WORD SEARCH

Romans

```
D E I F I T S U J B F G Q N Y E S H
N T D F Y K E X O G T K O L S L T V
M V W A C J A C N I I I D S I S U B
A K R L R X A O M N T R E V K E B T
H S E L E J R B I A A F I Q S X B P
A S T S M T U A N W N N S L N A O E
R I C H S S P M N O G W A L V T R C
B K H O G S E I C S R O D Z A X N C
A D E R M D T E A Y C C O M A V N A
B Y D T N I L C D E T F A R G P E K
A N O O N E R I G H T E O U S E S S
F E C G S I V Z O U S T B U O D S U
C O E F F R B R A N C H E S B O V L
N S R I E E L B I S I V N I H S J L
T H C S J N Q E B E O H P P G E N A
A E C A I D E M A H S A T O N G N C
S U R S Y M G N I N A O R G W A S E
E N A C R E D I T S N T Q Z R W C U
```

Two words have been chosen from each of the 16 chapters of Romans. These are the 32 words in this Word Search. As an extra game, figure out which words come from which chapter.

ABRAHAM
ACCEPT
BRANCHES
CALL
COALS
CONFESS
CREDITS
DOUBTS
FALL SHORT
GRAFTED
GROANING

INVISIBLE
INWARDLY
JACOB
JUSTIFIED
KISS
LIVING SACRIFICES
MERCY
NO CONDEMNATION
NO ONE RIGHTEOUS
NOT ASHAMED
PHOEBE

RESCUE
SIN
SLAVES
SPAIN
STRONG
STUBBORNNESS
SUBMIT
TAXES
WAGES
WRETCHED

WORD SEARCH

Ephesians

```
E R O M Y L B A R U S A E M M I U E
Y C R U E C O A R S E J O K I N G C
L H I L N L W W B S Y D O B I C K O
A I A L D W P G D L M J C T E O E N
H E E A A O H M R E E L Y R E M C T
T F H W R R G O E A P S A K H P A I
A C T G M F A E L T C O S S Y A E N
R O F N O Q F D K E Y E S E P R P U
W R O I R P A O I I S L B I D A F A
F N M D L X K I T A L O O O T B O L
O E O I W O R K S U N E M H X L D L
S R D V S N E I L A P T B E E Y N U
T S G I D E N I T S E D E R P G O S
C T N D P I H S N A M K R O W R B T
E O I Y L L U F H T U R T K A E P S
J N K P J N G N I E E T N A R A U G
B E R I C H I N M E R C Y Z X T L M
O D L R O W S I H T F O S Y A W C N
```

Find these words written by Paul in the book of Galatians in the puzzle on the opposite page.

ALIENS
ARMOR
BE LIKE GOD
BLESSED
BODY
BOND OF PEACE
CHIEF CORNERSTONE
COARSE JOKING
CONTINUAL LUST
DEPOSIT

DIVIDING WALL
GRACE
GUARANTEEING
HOLY TEMPLE
IMMEASURABLY MORE
INCOMPARABLY GREAT
KINGDOM OF THE AIR
OBEY
OBJECTS OF WRATH
PREDESTINED

PSALMS
PUT-OFF
RADIANT
RICH IN MERCY
SPEAK TRUTHFULLY
UNITY
UNWHOLESOME
WAYS OF THIS WORLD
WORKMANSHIP
WORKS

WORD SEARCH

Titus

```
Q S Z X J U G M A L I G N C A U C K
U O Y T I R G E T N I O R E Y W A L
R U N E T H G I A R T S T F C R S I
E N S V Z T U A P P O I N T E D J S
G D O E C R E T E O D E P R A W N R
A N Q S T Y N M B Q R E D L E O B E
E E F U E A F I P L D L I W I I E B
T S A P I T R I W E A O W S Y L P U
A S D R R C U E R A R M S A B V O K
L O D I E Q K R D U S A E A M E H E
K F I V N E W T B I P H T L G V D X
E S C E E C S T E Y S I I E E A E R
R P T N W N U R L M P N L N Y S S E
S E E E A S C D E S P O O S G E S B
N E D A L N L S O V V E P C Z Q E I
C C T Z C R A H G E O O R V Z O L R
T H E C O S E R I O U S N E S S B T
R R I W E L B A E C A E P L D U Z H
```

Find these words in the puzzle on the opposite page.

ADDICTED
APPOINTED
BLAMELESS
BLESSED HOPE
BRUTES
CONSIDERATE
CRETE
EAGER
ELDER
HOSPITABLE
INTEGRITY

LAWYER
LOVE
MALIGN
OVERSEER
PEACEABLE
PURIFY
QUICK-TEMPERED
REBIRTH
REBUKE
RENEWAL
SERIOUSNESS

SOUNDNESS OF
 SPEECH
STRAIGHTEN
TALKERS
TEMPERATE
WARPED
WASHING
WILD
WORLDLY PASSIONS

WORD SEARCH

James

```
Z L L I W S D R O L E H T D S P N K
E F I L F O N W O R C L P E P Q S A
G K T X B S R I D F L G S F A T H E
H A N A D O D E M E H I P T R O I P
P D H E R D V E W S A C R C K S F S
E A H R T I O U D R I I O K F S T O
R H I T E S O W P N A T R N T E I T
F M C C L Y I F H L I E I I F D N W
E W E L H I O L S A W M U R R E G O
C D A S R S F Z O O T R E E O Q S L
T K I V G U Q L L T F I L L L V H S
G W D N S X D F A T K I T P B O A I
I M O O I W D D S R G C A S G U D F
F S O U U L E R E I O U I E A G O P
T C B D I B I W O R U M R U R Y W D
B Z I W S F T N E L I J A H Q R S K
C S T H G I L Y L N E V A E H I O L
J P S X Y I W J O D E T U L L O P R
```

James writes like an Old Testament prophet. He uses crisp language and vivid imagery, and he's not shy about saying what he thinks. So he talks about mirrors and rudders and horse's bits. And he's not above mocking those who read God's Word but don't obey it—or those who see someone in need and pass by, saying, "I wish you well."

BITS
CONFESS
CROWN OF LIFE
DECEIVED
DOUBLE-MINDED
DOUBT
DO WHAT IT SAYS
ELIJAH
ERROR
FAVORITISM

FIRST FRUITS
HEAVENLY LIGHTS
I WISH YOU WELL
MIRROR
MORAL FILTH
PERFECT GIFT
POLLUTED
QUICK TO LISTEN
RAHAB
RELIGION

RUDDER
SHIFTING SHADOWS
SLOW TO SPEAK
SONGS OF PRAISE
SPARK
THE LORD'S WILL
TOSSED
TRIALS
WILD FLOWER
WISDOM

Section 2

puzzles, etc.

MATCHING

For these puzzles, you must draw a line from an item on the left side to its matching item on the right side. Each answer can be used only once. Be careful—some are tricky.

Creation

On which day of creation did God do each of these things? Match each day with that day's activity.

1. Made the sun, moon, and stars

2. Blessed this day and rested

3. Made the sky above and the water below

4. Formed the light and divided it from the darkness

5. Caused the dry land to appear and to bring forth plants

6. Caused the earth to bring forth every kind of animal and made man and woman

7. Filled the oceans with fish and the skies with birds

a. First day

b. Second day

c. Third day

d. Fourth day

e. Fifth day

f. Sixth day

g. Seventh day

MATCHING

—

Events in the Life of . . .

Which person did which thing? Match the Bible character with the correct event.

1. Eve
2. Noah
3. Jacob
4. Joseph
5. Moses
6. Balaam
7. David
8. Solomon
9. Elijah
10. Jonah
11. Daniel
12. Jesus

a. Killed Goliath

b. Parted the Red Sea

c. Ate the forbidden fruit

d. Was swallowed by a great fish

e. Ascended to heaven in a flaming chariot

f. Built God's temple in Jerusalem

g. Was thrown into a den of lions

h. Dreamed of a staircase reaching to heaven

i. His donkey spoke to him

j. Walked on water

k. Was thrown into a pit by his brothers

l. Built a big boat to escape a flood

MATCHING

■

Couples

Who was married to whom? Match each husband with his wife.

1.	Abigail	a.	Abraham
2.	Bathsheba	b.	Adam
3.	Elizabeth	c.	Ahab
4.	Eve	d.	Boaz
5.	Hannah	e.	David
6.	Jezebel	f.	Elkanah
7.	Mary	g.	Isaac
8.	Rachel	h.	Jacob
9.	Rahab	i.	Joseph
10.	Rebekah	j.	Moses
11.	Ruth	k.	Nabal
12.	Sarah	l.	Salmon
13.	Zipporah	m.	Zechariah

MATCHING

■

Parents and Children

Which child belonged to which parent?

1.	Abraham	a.	Abimelech
2.	Ahaz	b.	Cain
3.	Bathsheba	c.	David
4.	Eve	d.	Ham
5.	Gideon	e.	Hezekiah
6.	Hannah	f.	Ishmael
7.	Isaac	g.	Jacob
8.	Jehoshaphat	h.	Jehu
9.	Jesse	i.	Jonathan
10.	Leah	j.	Joseph
11.	Noah	k.	Joshua
12.	Nun	l.	Reuben
13.	Rachel	m.	Samuel
14.	Saul	n.	Solomon

MATCHING

Occupations

Who did what? Match the person with his or her job.

1. Abel
2. Boaz
3. David
4. Deborah
5. Eleazar
6. Elijah
7. Ezra
8. Ishmael
9. Jezebel
10. Joash
11. Joseph, Jesus' father
12. Joshua
13. Paul

a. Archer, hunter
b. Assistant to Moses
c. Carpenter
d. High priest
e. Judge
f. King
g. Musician, shepherd, and king
h. Prophet
i. Queen
j. Scribe
k. Shepherd
l. Tentmaker, missionary
m. Wealthy farmer

MATCHING

Where, Oh, Where?

Where did these events take place? Match each thing with its location.

1. Jesus was born.

2. Noah's ark landed.

3. The Israelites wandered for 40 years.

4. Plagued with frogs, lice, flies, hail, and other disasters

5. Moses received the Ten Commandments.

6. Joshua addressed Israel for the last time.

7. Jesus told his disciples about the end times.

8. Jesus grew up.

9. Jesus rode into the city on a donkey.

10. Jonah preached and the people repented.

a. Bethlehem

b. Egypt

c. Jerusalem

d. Mount Ararat

e. Mount of Olives

f. Mount Sinai

g. Nazareth

h. Nineveh

i. Shechem

j. The wilderness (Sinai desert)

MATCHING

■

I Say to You

Jesus said all these sayings on the left. But to whom was he speaking? Match the saying with the person(s) who first heard it.

1. "Before the rooster crows, you will disown me three times" (John 13:38).

2. "Didn't you know I had to be in my Father's house?" (Luke 2:49).

3. "Do not put the Lord your God to the test" (Matt. 4:7).

4. "Follow me" (Luke 5:27).

5. "I will make you fishers of men" (Mark 1:17).

6. "No one can see the kingdom of God unless he is born again" (John 3:3).

7. "Take your mat and go home" (Mark 2:11).

8. "Your faith has healed you" (Mark 10:52).

a. Bartimaeus

b. The devil

c. Levi (also known as Matthew)

d. Mary and Joseph

e. Nicodemus

f. The paralyzed man

g. Peter

h. Simon (Peter) and Andrew

MATCHING

Brothers and Sisters

Who was related to whom? Match the people at the left with their brothers (or half brothers) or sisters at the right.

1.	David	a.	Absalom
2.	Isaac	b.	Andrew
3.	Jacob	c.	Benjamin
4.	John	d.	Esau
5.	Joseph	e.	Ishmael
6.	Martha	f.	James
7.	Moses	g.	Lazarus
8.	Peter	h.	Leah
9.	Rachel	i.	Miriam
10.	Solomon	j.	Shammah

MATCHING

■

What Does It Say?

Which book of the Bible contains what stuff? Match the book to the proper description of what's in it.

1. Acts

2. Exodus

3. Genesis

4. Isaiah

5. Joshua

6. Matthew

7. Proverbs

8. Psalms

9. Revelation

10. Romans

a. Paul's presentation of what Christians believe

b. Predictions about the Servant-Messiah who would come

c. Songs of praise, requests for help, honest doubts

d. Story of beginnings of the earth and Israel

e. Story of Jesus' life and death

f. Story of the early church

g. Story of the Israelites' entry into Canaan

h. Story of the Israelites' escape from Egypt

i. Visions of the end times

j. Wise sayings

MATCHING

How Much?

Match each amount with the proper item.

1. 5

2. 7

3. 10

4. 12

5. 13

6. 20

7. 30

8. 40

9. 70

10. 5,000

a. Commandments

b. Days it rained in the Great Flood

c. Days of creation (including rest)

d. People miraculously fed once by Jesus

e. Pieces of silver paid for Joseph

f. Pieces of silver paid to Judas

g. Stones David picked up to slay Goliath with

h. Times Israelites marched around Jericho

i. Tribes of Israel

j. Years Israelites held captive in Babylon

HIDDEN WORDS

———————————— ■ ————————————

In the Hidden Words puzzles, you take the letters of the word we give you and rearrange some of these letters to form new words. Each letter can be used only once for each time it appears in the original word. For instance, if we give you *LETTER*, you could form the word *TREE* because there are two *E*'s. But you could not form *TELL* because you only have one *L* to work with.

(Hint: Try using Scrabble letters. First, form the original word. Then use those letter-tiles to form new words.)

This can be a great group or family activity, too. Be sure to write down all the words you come up with on a separate sheet of paper. It's impossible to keep track of them all in your head. (And it's best to put your list of words in columns according to their first letter. That'll keep you from duplicating.)

As you can see, the following puzzles increase in difficulty. That is, our "target scores" go up and up.

———————————— **1** ————————————

How many words can you find hidden in the letters of:

AHIMELECH

Ahimelech was the name of several Bible characters, including a priest in the time of David.

We found 23 words in this name, and there have to be even more than that. Can you beat our score?

———————————— **2** ————————————

How many words can you find hidden in the letters of:

DEBORAH

Deborah was a prophetess and judge in Israel after the time of Joshua.

We found 32 words in her name, and there may even be more than that. Can you beat our score?

HIDDEN WORDS

3

How many words can you find hidden in the letters of:

MATTHEW

Matthew was a tax collector who became a disciple of Jesus. He also wrote the first Gospel.

We found 38 words in his name, and there may even be more than that. Can you beat our score?

4

How many words can you find hidden in the letters of:

JEHOSHAPHAT

Jehoshaphat was the king of Judah in the time of Elijah.

We found 53 words in his name, and there may even be more than that. Can you beat our score?

5

How many words can you find hidden in the letters of:

MESOPOTAMIA

Mesopotamia is the name for the region between the Tigris and Euphrates Rivers (where Iraq is now). Abraham originally came from this area, and the Israelites were taken there in captivity for 70 years.

We found 57 words in the name of this place, and we know there must be more than that. Can you beat our score?

HIDDEN WORDS

6

How many words can you find hidden in the letters of:

NEBUCHADNEZZAR

Nebuchadnezzar was king of Babylon when the Jews were taken captive. Daniel served in his administration.
We found 73 words, and there may even be more than that. Can you beat our score?

7

How many words can you find hidden in the letters of:

APOSTLES

"Apostles" was the name given to the first disciples of Jesus, as well as Paul and other missionaries of the early church.
We found 76 words in this title, and there may even be more than that. Can you beat our score?

8

How many words can you find hidden in the letters of:

THESSALONIANS

Thessalonians lived in Thessalonica, in the northern area of Greece. The apostle Paul visited this church and wrote it two letters.
We found 87 words in the letters of this word, and there may be more than that. Can you beat our score?

HIDDEN WORDS

9

How many words can you find hidden in the letters of:

REVELATION

Revelation is the last book of the Bible, a collection of visions about the end times written by the apostle John.

We found 140 words in this book's name, and there may even be more than that. Can you beat our score?

10

How many words can you find hidden in the letters of:

BARTHOLOMEW

Bartholomew was a disciple of Jesus.

We found 142 words in his name, and there could be more than that. Can you beat our score?

CRISSCROSS

We give you the words. Just fit them into the diagram. You'll need to count the letters and compare words to see which ones fit best.

1

Old Testament Characters

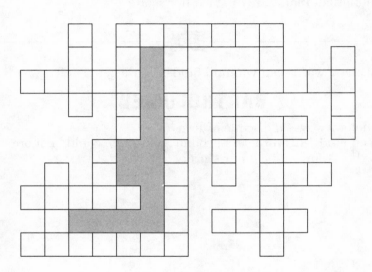

3-Letter names
Asa
Eve
Lot

4-letter names
Adam
Boaz
Cain
Ezra
Noah

5-letter names
Aaron
Jacob
Jonah
Moses

6-letter names
Isaiah
Jethro

7-letter names
Ezekiel
Jezebel

10-letter names
Zerubbabel

Journeys of Paul

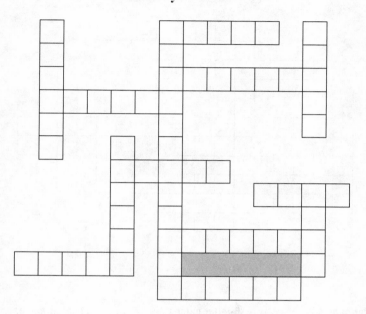

4-letter names
Myra
Rome

5-letter names
Assos
Malta
Perga
Troas

6-letter names
Arabia
Lystra
Smyrna
Tarsus

7-letter names
Ephesus
Iconium

12-letter names
Thessalonica

CRISSCROSS

Kings of Judah and Israel

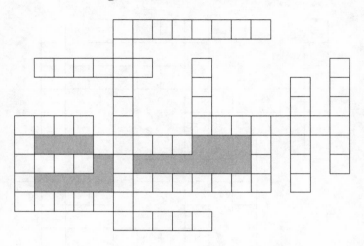

4-letter names
Ahab
Ahaz
Elah
Jehu

5-letter names
Joash
Nadab
Tibni

6-letter names
Abijam
Baasha
Hoshea
Jotham

8-letter names
Hezekiah
Jeroboam
Zedekiah

11-letter names
Jehoshaphat

CRISSCROSS

4

Judges of Israel

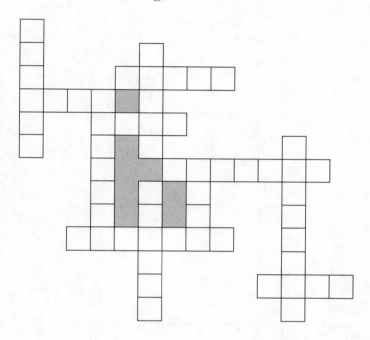

4-letter names
Ehud
Elon
Jair
Tola

5-letter names
Abdon
Ibzan

6-letter names
Gideon
Samson

7-letter names
Deborah
Othniel
Shamgar

8-letter names
Jephthah

CRISSCROSS

5

New Testament Characters

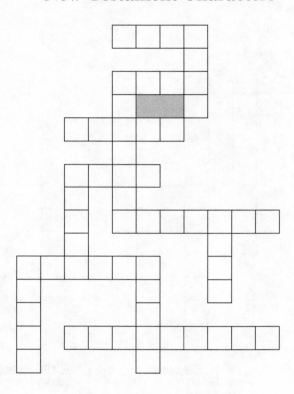

4-letter names
John
Luke
Mark
Mary
Paul

5-letter names
Herod
James
Jesus
Peter

6-letter names
Joseph

7-letter names
Matthew
Wise Men

9-letter names
Nicodemus

CRISSCROSS

Tribes of Israel

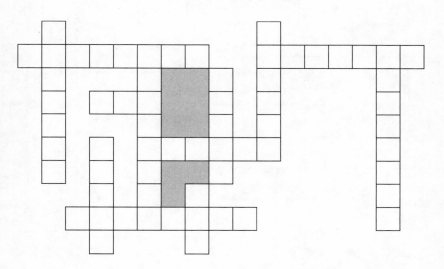

3-Letter names
Dan
Gad

5-letter names
Asher
Judah

6-letter names
Reuben
Simeon

7-letter names
Ephraim
Zebulun

8-letter names
Benjamin
Issachar
Manasseh
Naphtali

CRISSCROSS

7

Ephesians

3-Letter words
Day
Old
Sun

4-Letter words
Dead
Hope
Know
Rage
Self
Sins

5-Letter words
Fills
Kneel
Realm
Songs
Steal
Waves

6-Letter words
Aliens
Malice
Rooted
Spirit

7-Letter words
Adopted
Barrier
Fathers
Infants
Sleeper
Wrinkle

8-Letter words
Approach
Ascended
Darkness
Fragrant
Gentiles

9-Letter words
Hostility
Ignorance
Reverence

10-Letter words
Foreigners
Sufferings

11-Letter words
Enlightened
Regulations

CRISSCROSS

8

1 Timothy

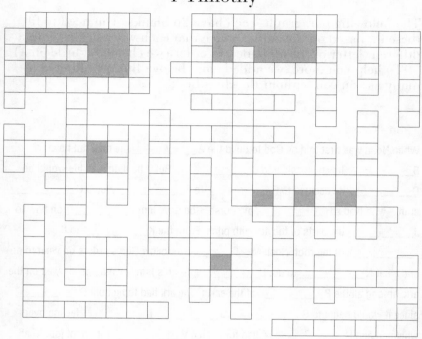

3-Letter words
Age
Eve
Son

Letter words
Adam
Asia
Gain
Rash
Wine

5-Letter words
Crops
Guard
Hasty
Judge
Money
Myths
Teach
Truth

6-Letter words
Delude
Herald
Strong

7-Letter words
Abandon
Abusive
Ephesus
Eternal
Neglect
Pierced
Soldier
Violent

8-Letter words
Civilian
Depraved
Impostor

9-Letter words
Arguments
Enjoyment
Propriety
Reminding

10-Letter words
Conscience

11-Letter words
Immortality
Trustworthy

ALPHAGRAPHS

Flood Preparations

The following paragraphs each have 26 blanks. You need to fill these in, based on the story. Notice that each word begins with a different letter of the alphabet, in order (we cheated a little on *X*).

To help you more, we added clues below. But try filling in as many as you can without the clues first.

When Noah was first told by God to build the A_____, he may not have B_____ it was possible to C_____ it. But if he didn't, all life would be D_____. He decided to E_____ to F_____ such a G_____ craft—with God's H_____, of course. God gave him I_____ on how to J_____ the parts of the ark with pitch. From the K_____ to the L_____ of the roof, Noah M_____ to follow God's orders on what to do and what N_____ to do. O_____ Noah's family would be allowed on the ark, among all the P_____ of the earth. The ark had to be built Q_____, since it would begin to R_____ S_____. T_____ feeling over-whelmed and U_____-qualified for such a V_____ important job, Noah built the ark before the W_____ rose. He must have been eX_____ by the time it was finished, Y_____ he didn't stop until the last Z_____ was on board.

A. Boat	K. Boat part	T. Considering that
B. Trusted	L. What you kiss with	U. Below
C. Build	M. Oversaw, or was	V. Much
D. Ruined	capable	W. Liquids
E. Attempt	N. Shoelace in a tangle	X. Tired
F. Shape	O. Alone	Y. But
G. Huge, or very good	P. Humans	Z. Striped beast
H. Assistance	Q. In a rush	
I. Teachings	R. Precipitation	
J. Become a member	S. In a short time	
of, or affix		

ALPHAGRAPHS

Beginnings

A_____ and Eve lived in the B_____ Garden of Eden, which God had

C_____ for them. Their D_____ was caused by E_____'s desire to

taste the F_____ F_____ from the tree of the knowledge of G_____

and evil. H_____, God did not destroy them, but I_____ banished them

from the Garden. As always, God was J_____ in his judgment.

   Although he K_____ them out of the Garden, God L_____ the

M_____ and woman settle elsewhere. N_____ O_____ else was

yet in existence, so Adam and Eve decided to become P_____ and Q_____

had Cain and Abel. Cain was a farmer and R_____ crops, while Abel was a

S_____. T_____ they worked side by side U_____ each gave a

gift to the Lord. The result was not V_____ brotherly! It makes you

W_____ how brothers can get along with each other. Eve may have wished she

did not have the mixture of _____ and _____ chromosomes to have these

two boys. Cain, especially, seemed to be a Z_____.

A. First guy
B. Lovely
C. Made
D. Doom
E. Mother of all living
F. Banned/Banana,
   for instance
G. Righteousness
H. Yet
I. In its place

J. Right, or only
K. Held, or prevented
L. Allow
M. Dog's best friend
N. Negative
O. Three divided by
   three
P. Ma and Pa
Q. Zippily
R. Lifted
S. Tender of woolies

T. As one
U. Up to the time that
V. Greatly
W. Consider, doubt
X. Name for a
   collection of genes
Y. A health club, for
   short
Z. Three minus three

ALPHAGRAPHS

Down Time (twice through)

A_____ embarrassing the prophets of B_____ at Mount C_____, the prophet of God was D_____. His name was E_____. Suddenly he had to F_____ the wrath of the G_____ queen. When she H_____ the news, she was I_____. Her name was J_____, the wife of the weak-kneed K_____ Ahab.

With his L_____ on the line, Elijah fled to a desert M_____. N_____ could cheer him up. As he looked O_____ his life, he was full of self-P_____. Despite his triumphs, that wicked Q_____ was still R_____ to kill him. He just S_____ and moped. "T_____ my life," he prayed, U_____ dejected. His recent V_____ was now just a memory.

Then God said, "W_____ are you doing here?"

Elijah was eX_____ and replied, "How can Y_____ ask me that? I have been very Z_____ for you, Lord, and A_____ I get is trouble. The people have B_____ down your altars, they are C_____ on Baal to save them, and now they want to put me to D_____."

God sent a mighty wind. Then he made a violent E_____ shake the place. Then he sent a F_____ to burn all around Elijah. But, the Bible says, the Lord was not in those mighty things. Then God spoke in a G_____ whisper. "What are you doing H_____?" he asked again.

Elijah was I_____ in the lesson God was teaching him, but the queen was still J_____ of him—he K_____ that much. He L_____ for the voice, but he heard only the M_____ of the breeze. N_____ he began to understand what he O_____ was deaf to. God can speak in P_____ ways, as he did on Mount Carmel, but he usually speaks Q_____. Elijah R_____ that the S_____, S_____ voice was guiding him. It T_____ him to get U_____ and go to Syria V_____ the desert. There he W_____ anoint a new king. Hey, this was getting to be eX_____! He would also anoint a new prophet. Y_____, his life would have more Z_____ from now on!

194

ALPHAGRAPHS

Down Time (twice through) (cont.)

A. Following
B. False god
C. Biblical mountain
D. Saddened, blue
E. A famous prophet
F. Run away
G. Atheistic
H. Got word of
I. Angered, or perfumed
J. A wicked queen
K. Monarch
L. Existence
M. Alp, for instance
N. Not one iota
O. Above
P. Compassion
Q. Esther was one
R. Prepared
S. Had a seat
T. Wrest
U. Totally
V. Win?
W. Huh?
X. Frustrated, hopeless
Y. Second person
Z. Excited, faithful

A. Everything
B. Smashed, dismantled
C. Summoning
D. Expiration
E. The Richter scale measures it
F. Flame
G. Soft
H. This place
I. Engaged, "into"
J. Envious
K. Recognized
L. Paid attention to
M. Muttering, whimpering
N. This time
O. That time
P. Mighty
Q. Silently, softly
R. Came to know
S. Motionless/Tiny
T. Said
U. Risen
V. By way of
W. Was expected to, a helping verb
X. Thrilling
Y. Affirmative
Z. Joy, or a deodorant soap

CODES

The following paragraph contains a Bible verse, but there's a trick to reading it. Circle the first letter and cross out the second, then circle the next and cross out the next, all the way through the puzzle. Then, just read the circled letters.

```
D G O T N L O X T S J M U Q D O G Y E B A K N R D C Y U O H U F W Z
I V L A L U N I O E T P B D E F J K U A D H G I E L D K D J O F N D O R
T S C X O V N A D J E I M Q N W A H N A D B Y O O P U L W Z I K L L
L O N I O R T S B D E F C L O V N Y D A E J M T N Z E H D Q F W O M
R S G E I T V O E K A P N T D O Y B O C U K W L I W L S L M B Q E H
F V O L R A G P I Z V K E R N P G A I J V T E X A Y N F D G I L T S W U
I R L A L I B C E D G S I M V J E N N W T K O B Y D O J U R
```

_____

_____

_____

_____

CODES

2

This is a *different* code. The key to solving it is printed upside down, but see if you can figure it out yourself. Hint: The first word is *Shout.*)

```
S D E H X P O B Y U J Z T L R F M A O C K R G V J K E O F P Y D L T K
M O W S T P B H Z C E Y F L D T O M G R X F D B Z A E R L P W L K B
T Y M H S X E C V E K D A F L R B V T Q X H A E W J R O Y N R U B S
G P H G F I M K P Q V T B J H W S E Z C L M B O K F R F A D T N W E
L I U H T P K H Y G G X S L I F A N E D W R N G S E M X S Q A S C N
C P Z O B I M D W E G K B F T E R S F V H O X E R T D E Y B H V X I D
Y M E U W Q H I W X T K G H X V J N D O I W Y M B F E T U T Y L M
W S L C O P F N M D G T R S
```

_____

_____

_____

_____

Key to Code #2: Start with the first letter (*S*) and circle every *third* letter, crossing out the next two.

197

CODES

3

This is the hardest code yet. Sometimes you skip one letter, sometimes two. Can you figure it out? Hint: the first word is *The*, and the second word is another word for *rock*. The key to this code is upside down.

T B H F E G Z S J T Q O R V N K E M P T W H N E L X B C U K R I W Y
L J D S E T D R O S F R B E O G J F E K L C V T Q E K J D P H F A B G
S N B M E W Y C F O T Z M F E U X T G H C E B J C M A P T P R S B T
F O H K N A E D J T B H P E V Z L C O S F R Q D M H J A T S S L D B O
C F N H E P R T P H B I C D S R A K H N Q D E I C B T F I R S S G M E
A D J R G V I E B D L F O G N U H Z S K I P M N B O L V U C K R D E J
M Y G E T H S.

_____

_____

_____

_____

Key to Code #3: If the letter you just circled is a vowel (A, E, I, O, U, and *not* Y this time), cross out the next two letters and circle the next. If you just circled a consonant, cross out just the next letter and then circle the next. Vowel, skip two; consonant, skip one.

ALPHACODES

Let's invent a new alphabet. Then let's see if you can figure out the missing words in the verses below.

Alphabet 1

A = ?	B = %	C = #	D = @
E = >	F = &	G = \	H = <
I = +	J = !	K = (	L =)
M = "	N = /	O = '	P = :
Q = ;	R = -	S = 7	T = $
U = 3	V = {	W = }	X = 4
Y = 2	Z = 8		

Verse A

Trust in the)'-@ with all your <>?-$ and)>?/ /'$ on your own 3 /@ >-7$?/@+/ \; in all your }?27 acknowledge him, and he will "?(> your paths 7$-?+\<$ (Proverbs 3:5-6).

_____

_____

_____

_____

_____

_____

Alphabet 1 (cont.)

Verse B

Our &?$<>-, who art in <>?{>/, Hallowed be thy /?">. Thy (+/\
@'" come, Thy }+)) be @'/>, on <?-$< as it is in <>?{>/. Give
us this @?2 our @?+)2 %->?@, and &'-\+{> us our $->7:?77>7,
as we &'-\+{> those who $->7:?77 against us. And)>?@ us not
into $>":$?$+'/, but @>)+{>- us from >{+), for thine is the (+/\
@'" and the :'}>- and the \)'-2 forever and >{>-. Amen
(Matthew 6:9-13).

_____

_____

_____

_____

The verse above is a famous prayer taught by Jesus. Many
churches say it regularly in their worship services. But the
thoughts and feelings are more important than the exact words.

Does prayer seem like a puzzle to you? Do you feel that there's
some secret code that you have to know to get through to God?
That's not true at all! God longs to hear from you—about
anything. Tell God how your day is going, how you feel about
things, ask him to help you get through the tough stuff.

That's what this prayer is really all about.

Alphabet 2

Now let's try a whole new alphabet code.

A = 🐢   B = 🐕   C = 🌷   D = 🐟

E = 🐝   F = ☀   G = ☾   H = 🐟

I = 🪶   J = 🎤   K = ～   L = 🦎

M = 🎹   N = ∿   O = 👁   P = 🌴

Q = 🎻   R = 🐚   S = 〰   T = 🌿

U = 👒   V = 🥤   W = 🌺   X = 🍃

Y = 🦜   Z = ♫

Verse C

The 🌴🐢🐚🐕🦎🐝〰 of the 🐟🪶👁🐝🐝∿ 🌿🐚🐝🐢〰 👒🐚👁 and the 🌴🐢🐢👁🦜.

The ～🪶∿☾👁🐝🎹 of 🐟🐝🐢🥤🐝∿ is like 🌿🐚🐝🐢👒🐚👁 🐟🪶👁 in a ☀🪶🦎👁. When a man ☀🐝👒∿👁 it, he 🐟🪶👁 it again, and 🌿🐟🐝∿ in his 🪶🐝🦜 went and 〰👁🦎👁 all he had and 🐕🐝👒☾🐟🌿 that ☀🪶🐝🦎👁.

🐢☾🐢🪶∿, the ～🪶∿☾👁🐝🎹 of 🐟🐝🐢🥤🐝∿ is like a 🐕🐝🐚🍃🐟🐢∿🌿 looking for ☀🪶∿🐝 🌴🐢🐢👁🦜. When he 👒🐝∿👁 👁∿👁🐝 of great 🥤🐢🦎👒🐝, he went 🐢🌺🐢🦜 and sold 🐝🥤🐝🐚🦜🌿🪶🐟🪶∿☾ he had and 🐕🐝☾🐟🌿 🪶🌿.

(Matthew 13:44-46)

_____

_____

_____

Alphabet 2 (cont.)

Verse D

But when you ⟨symbols⟩ to the ⟨symbols⟩, do not let your ⟨symbols⟩ know what your ⟨symbols⟩ is doing, so that your ⟨symbols⟩ may be in ⟨symbols⟩. Then your ⟨symbols⟩, who ⟨symbols⟩ what is done in ⟨symbols⟩, will ⟨symbols⟩ you. (Matthew 6:3-4)

Alphabet 3

And, now that you're getting into this, let's try a third alphabet code.

A = ✹	B = ✪	C = ✳	D = ✷
E = ✸	F = ✾	G = ✴	H = ✳
I = ✳	J = ✳	K = ✳	L = ●
M = ○	N = ■	O = ❑	P = ❐
Q = ❑	R = ❏	S = ▲	T = ▼
U = ◆	V = ❖	W = ◗	X = I
Z = ▮			

Alphabet 3 (cont.)

Verse E

I ✳■❑◗ ◗✳✿▼ it is to be in ■✳✳✳ , and I ✳■❑◗
◗✳✿▼ it is to ✿✿❖✳ ❑●✳■▼I . I have ●✳✿❑■✳✳
the ▲✳✳❑✳▼ of being ✳❑■▼✳■▼ in ✿■I and every
▲✳▼◆✿▼✳❑■ . . . whether ●✳❖✳■✳ in ❑●✳■▼I
or in ◗✿■▼ . I can do ✳❖✳❑I▼✳✳■✳ through ✳✳○
who gives me ▲▼❑✳■✳▼✳ . (Philippians 4:12-13)

_____

_____

_____

_____

Verse F

Beyond all ❑◆✳▲▼✳❑■ , the ○I▲▼✳❑I of ✳❑✳●✳■✳▲▲
is great: He ✿❑❑✳✿❑✳✳ in a ✿❑✳I , was ❖✳■✳✳ -
✳✿▼✳✳ by the ▲❑✳❑✳▼ , was ▲✳✳■ by ✿■✳✳●▲ ,
was ❑❑✳✿✳✳✳✳ among the ■✿▼✳❑■▲ , was
✿✳●✳✳✳❖✳✳ on in the ◗❑●✳ , was ▼✿✳✳■ ◆❑ in
✳●❑❑I . (1 Timothy 3:16)

_____

_____

_____

_____

_____

MAZES

Wild Ones

On Moses' journey through the wilderness, he must pass through the Red Sea (RS), gather some manna to eat (M), and collect the two stone tablets with the Ten Commandments (10C). As you solve this maze, you must go through all those spots before you reach the land of Israel (I).

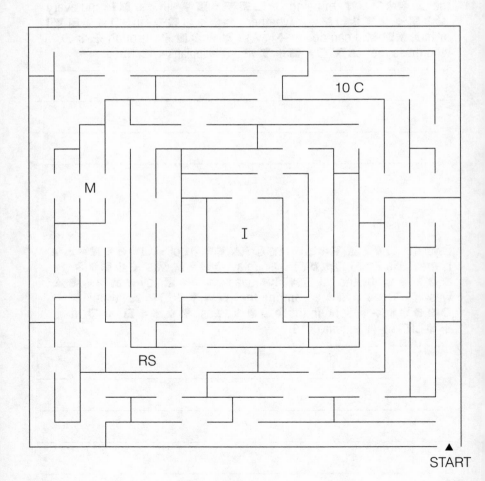

START

MAZES

■

Christmas Shopping

The three wise men are going on a journey to visit the baby Jesus. On the way, each must pass through a particular spot to pick up a gift for Jesus. Caspar must start from where he is (C) and pick up the gift of gold (G) before visiting Jesus (J). Melchior (M) must pick up the frankincense (F), and Balthasar (B) must pick up the myrrh (M). They may cross each other's path or even share the road for a while, but they must not find each other's gifts. One wise man's path is simple, but the other two take more twists and turns.

(Hint: You may try to do all three at once, or do the maze three different times—but be sure to use a *pencil*, so you can erase if you have to.)

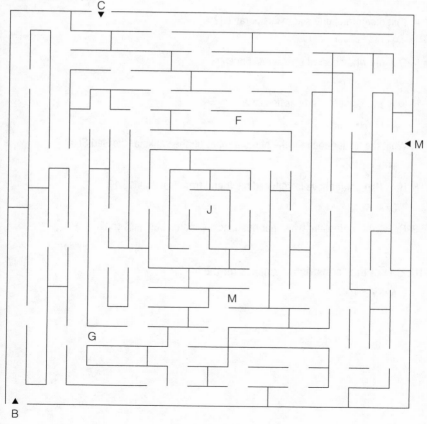

HANKY-PANKY

Each of the following clues has a two-part answer, and the two parts rhyme. Example: Peter as a poet—"Rhymin' Simon," or Jericho's disaster—"Wall Fall."

1. What Jacob did when he met with his brother?

   H* S** E***

2. What you do when you need an apostle?

   C*** P***

3. What the writer of the next to last NT book was called by the people he insulted?

   R*** J***

4. That dangerous guy whom Jesus raised?

   H******** L******

5. The guy who cheered up Xerxes' queen?

   E*****'s J*****

6. Why Eve couldn't find her fig leaves?

   A*** H** 'em

7. What the leader does for the photographer on the banks of the Red Sea?

   M**** P****

8. How Paul might have introduced his friend from Romans 16:1?

   S** B* P*****

9. Rebekah's complaint when her husband went on a business trip?

   I L*** I****

10. One of the "constrictor" snakes on the ark?

    N***'s B**

RHYME TIME

The following pairs of people had names that rhymed with each other's. Can you name them?

1. Woman who hid spies in Jericho; King who opposed Elijah

2. Israelite king; Christian apostle

3. Prophet who fathered Maher-Shalal-Hash-Baz; Prophet who fathered Lo-Ruhamah and Lo-Ammi

4. Leader of Persian Empire who released the Jews from captivity; Jewish official whose son was raised by Jesus

5. King who had 15 years added to his life; Prophet who bemoaned the fall of Jerusalem

6. Son of Abraham; Jacob's new name

Each of the following circles gives you a glimpse of some passage of the Bible (New International Version). Can you figure out what book of the Bible each glimpse is from?

You may want to look for words from familiar verses or names (or partial names) that you might recognize. Feel free to use your own Bible to help you locate these mystery circles.

1

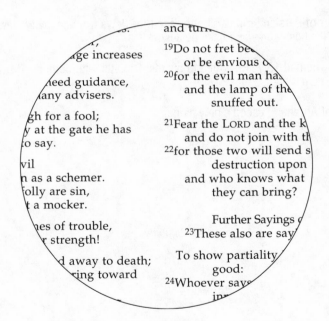

```
                    and tur
  ge increases    ¹⁹Do not fret be
                     or be envious o
  eed guidance,   ²⁰for the evil man ha
  any advisers.      and the lamp of th
                        snuffed out.
  gh for a fool;
  y at the gate he has   ²¹Fear the LORD and the k
  o say.              and do not join with t
                   ²²for those two will send s
  vil                    destruction upon
  n as a schemer.     and who knows what
  olly are sin,          they can bring?
  t a mocker.
                        Further Sayings o
  es of trouble,    ²³These also are say
  r strength!
                   To show partiality
  d away to death;        good:
  ing toward      ²⁴Whoever say
                          in
```

2

wn mercy.
re in heart,
see God.
he peacemakers,
will be called sons of God.
are those who are persecuted
ecause of righteousness,
heirs is the kingdom of heaven.
ssed are you when people insult
ersecute you and falsely say all
of evil against you because of me.
e and be glad, because great is
ward in heaven, for in the same
ey persecuted the prophets who
ore you.

ht

e salt of the earth. Bit of
altiness, how can it be
no longer good for
n out and

surp
teachers
enter the k

Murder
21"You have hea
the people long a
and anyone who n
to judgment.' 22But
who is angry with
subject to judgment
says to his brother,
to the Sanhedrin. B
'You fool!' will be
hell.
23"Therefore
gift at the altar
your brother
24leave you
First g
er; t

3

ground.
majesty to
him,
his appearance that we
desire him.
spised and rejected by men,
of sorrows, and familiar with
ffering.
ne from whom men hide their
faces
was despised, and we esteemed
him not.

e took up our infirmities
arried our sorrows,
considered him stricken by God,
by him, and afflicted.
pierced for our
ressions,
hed for our iniquities;
that brought us peace

and
though he
nor was a
10Yet it was the
him and
and though th
a guilt of
he will see his off
his days,
and the will of
prosper in
11After the sufferi
he will see the
satisfied
by his knowled
serva
and he
12Therefo

4

¹The L
                        n
² He makes
                        pastu
he leads me
³ he restores
He guides me
                        righ
for his na
⁴Even th

raise

e him!
, honor

ts of

5

and   yo
hat you may live
land the Lord your
iving you.
ot murder.
ot commit adultery.
ot steal.
ot give false testimony
your neighbor.
ot cover your neigh-
e. You shall not cov-
bor's wife, or his
maidserv

2

Heb
2
ser
ye

6

you: You
ed in strip of
anger."
t company of the
ared with the angel,
aying,

the highest,
ace to men on
avor rests."

ad left them and
ephers said to
lehem and

upo
by th
before
²⁷Move
temple
in the c
custom
took hi
sayin
29

7

up, ¹⁵that e
may have etern
¹⁶"For God so
gave his one and o
believes in him sha
eternal life. For G
Son into the wor
world but to sav
him. ¹⁸Whoever
condemned, but
lieve stands

ʎi-
was

Phari-
nber of
e to
w

8

phets testify.
om God comes
s Christ to all who
o difference, ²³for all
fall short of the glory of
justified freely by his
the redemption that came
us. ²⁵God presented him as
atonement, through faith in
e did this to demonstrate his
use in his forbearance he had
committed beforehand un-
⁶he did it to demonstrate his
resent time, so as to be just
o justifies the man who
sus.
is boasting? It is ex-
rinciple? On that of
o, but on that of
that a man is
ving

of the
eousness a

⁷"Blessed are th
whose transg
whose sins are
⁸Blessed is the man
whose sin the Lor
against him."

⁹Is this blessedness
cumcised, or also for t
We have been saying
faith was credited to
ness. ¹⁰Under what c
credited? Was it afte
cised, or before? It
fore! ¹¹And he re
circumcision, a
that he had
uncircu

ng, live for-
angel, and he
lions. They have
was found inno-
have I ever done
, O king."
joyed and gave or-
of the den. And
from the den, no
n, because he

men

great
ent fror
sea.
4"The fi
the wings
wings wer
the groun
like a mar
given to
5"Ar
beas

10

will
er into
who carry

net ring off
aman son of
the enemy of
ey," the king
th the people

day of the
ies were
script

and
ashes.
4When Esth
came and told r
was in great dist
him to put on in
but he would not
ther summoned
king's eunuchs a
and ordered him
troubling Mord

6So Hathac
th open sq
king's

CHANGELINGS

In the following puzzles, the goal is to change the top word into the bottom word one letter at a time. At each step, you'll change one letter and possibly rearrange the letters to form a new word. Then you'll do the same with the letters of that word, until you reach your target word. To help you along, we've put definitions of the middle words to the right.

(Example: Turn HATE to LOVE. The *E* can stay. Change the *T* to a *V* and get HAVE. Change the *H* to an *L* and shuffle the letters to get VEAL. Then change the *A* to an *O* and shuffle to get LOVE. HATE-HAVE-VEAL-LOVE.)

1

Let's look at the books of the New Testament. Can you change MARK to LUKE? Both of them have a *K,* so we only need to change three other letters.

MARK	
* * * *	Create
* * * *	Body of water
LUKE	

2

Now let's go from Luke to the next book, John. This will be harder.

LUKE	
* * * *	Microwave something (slang)
* * * *	Wedding month
* * * *	Roman goddess
JOHN	

CHANGELINGS

And the next book has four letters, too. Let's go from John to Acts.

JOHN
* * * *   Kid around
* * * *   Writes down
* * * *   What Quaker Life is made of
ACTS

4

Proverbs 3:5 says, "TRUST in the Lord with all your HEART." Let's use those two key words in our next changeling puzzle. The *R* and a *T* can stay, but we'll need to change three other letters.

TRUST
* * * * *   Speak
* * * * *   Delight or surprise
HEART

5

In Isaiah 1:18, God promises that our SINS can be washed and made as white as SNOW or WOOL. Let's try those three words in our next changeling.

SINS
* * * *   Progeny
SNOW
* * * *   Snail-like
WOOL

PHONE FUN

━━━━━━━━━━━━ ■ ━━━━━━━━━━━━

Look at a telephone. Notice how certain numbers have letters
assigned to them. That's because, in the early days of telephones,
parts of phone numbers were spelled out with letters instead of
numbers. You still see this sometimes on advertisements.

Anyway, do you think you could read some key words in Bible
verses just from seeing their telephone numbers? It's not as easy
as it might seem, since each number has *three* possible letters that
could stand for it. You'll have to try different combinations to see
which letters fit together. Also, pay attention to the meaning of
the verse. That may help.

The Code:
2 = A, B, or C
3 = D, E, or F
4 = G, H, or I
5 = J, K, or L

6 = M, N, or O
7 = P, R, or S (note: Q is missing)
8 = T, U, or V
9 = W, X, or Y (note: Z is missing)

1. "Everyone who 22557 on the 6263 of the 5673 will be 72833."

_____

2. "I 5683 the 5673, for he 43273 my 86423."

_____

3. "7729 for each other so that 968 may be 432533."

_____

Praying is like calling God on the phone. A lot of people think
that praying has to be a big, formal event, where we pretend to be
really holy and pious. Well, it doesn't have to be like that. God
does want to be treated with respect, but he also likes to be
treated as a friend. And we call our friends all the time, right?
Why not take a moment right now, in your heart, to "call God
up" and say hi.

MYSTERY MATH

Some people hate math. If you're one of those people, skip over these next few puzzles. But others really like it. Here's a chance to put your Bible knowledge together with your math know-how.

Notice the "footnotes" in these problems. If you don't know the number off the top of your head, look it up in the reference provided.

Take the number of loaves plus the number of fish Jesus used in feeding the 5,000[A] ____ + ____ = ____

Add the number of chapters in Philippians +____ = ____

Subtract the number of people on board Noah's ark[B] - ____ = ____

Subtract the number of letters in the New Testament that were written to Timothy - ____ = ____

What is your final answer?

A. John 6:9
B. 1 Peter 3:20

MYSTERY MATH

2

Take the number of Commandments[A] plus the number of tribes of Israel[B] ____ + ____ = ____

Subtract the number of chapters in Romans - ____ = ____

Add the number of years the Israelites wandered in the wilderness[C] + ____ = ____

Subtract the number of "seals" in the book of Revelation[D] - ____ = ____

What is your final answer?

A. Exodus 20:1-17
B. Exodus 24:4
C. Deuteronomy 8:2
D. Revelation 6:1; 8:1

Take the number of books in the New Testament ____

Divide by the number of disciples who went with Jesus up the Mount of Transfiguration[A] ____ = ____

Multiply by the number of Old Testament figures with Jesus on the Mount of Transfiguration[B] x ____ = ____

Add the number of chapters in Proverbs + ____ = ____

Divide by the number of times Naaman had to wash in the Jordan River[C]

____ = ____

What is your final answer?

A. Matthew 17:1
B. Matthew 17:3
C. 2 Kings 5:10

MYSTERY MATH

Take the number of years Methusaleh lived[A] ____

Divide by the number of days Jonah was inside the great fish[B]
____ = ____

Add the number of days of creation (including the day of rest)[C]
+ ____ = ____

Subtract the age of Jesus when he began his ministry[D] - ____ = ____

Divide by the number of chapters in Genesis ____ = ____

Multiply by the number of people who passed by the injured man before

the Good Samaritan helped him[E] x ____ = ____

Add the number of brothers the Prodigal Son had[F] + ____ = ____

Subtract the number of lepers Jesus healed (when only one returned
to thank him)[G] - ____ = ____

What is your final answer?

A. Genesis 5:27
B. Jonah 1:17
C. Genesis 2:2
D. Luke 3:23
E. Luke 10:31-33
F. Luke 15:11
G. Luke 17:12

LINE-UPS

―――――――――――――――――――――――― ■ ――――――――――――――――――――――――

Here's a puzzle form that may be new to you. It's as if a quotation had been lined up in columns and all the letters dropped straight down, rearranged in alphabetical order. Your job is to move those letters back up into the proper spots in their columns, thus reassembling the quotation. Note that the text wraps from line to line. Unless there's a space at the end or beginning of a line, the same word continues on the next line. To help you a little, each puzzle indicates which book of the Bible the quotation is taken from.

Tips for solving: Look first at the lines with just two or three letters. They may be easiest to place. Then look at the small words in the diagram. Using the same sort of logic as with Cryptograms, try to drop some letters in. Look across the lines to see possible letter groups ("ING" or "TION") and to rule out letter-combinations that don't go together. Also look for unusual letters that are usually seen only in certain places ("J" usually starts a word) or with other letters ("K" preceding or following "N" or following "C").

As Isaiah said, "Precept must be upon precept . . . line upon line . . . here a little and there a little" (Isaiah 28:10, KJV). That's exactly the way to solve this—here a little, there a little—and I hope you gain a few precepts as you reconstruct the lines.

LINE-UP

Numbers

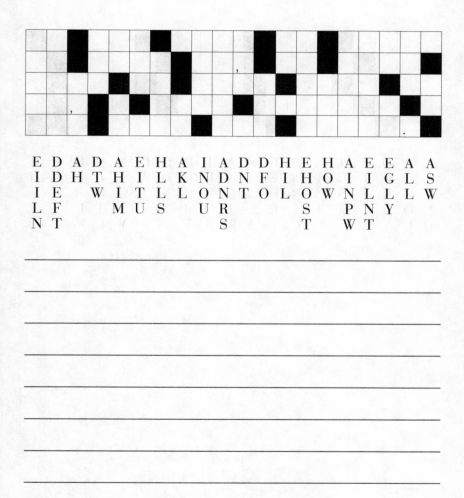

LINE-UP

Deuteronomy

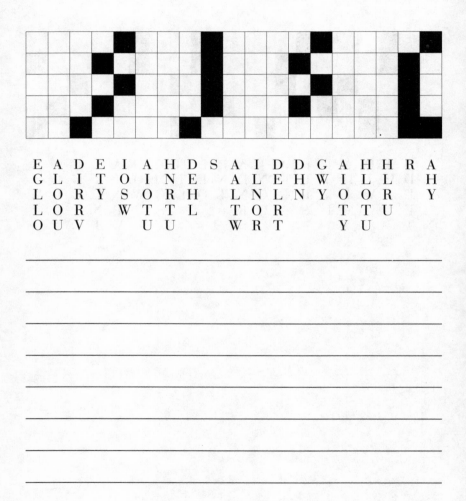

LINE-UP

Ruth

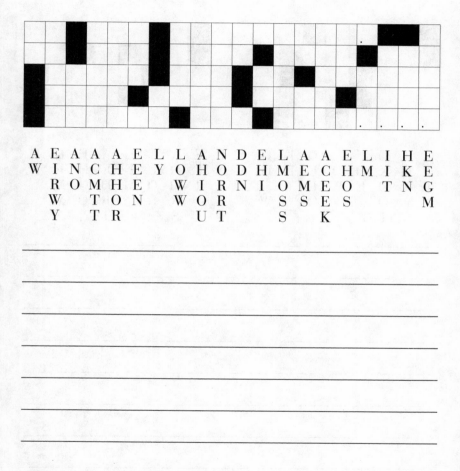

A E A A A E L L A N D E L A A E L I H E
W I N C H E Y O H O D H M E C H M I K E
R O M H E   W I R N I O E E O   T N G
W   T O N   W O R T   S M S S   S   M
Y   T R   U T   S S E K

LINE - UP

2 Samuel

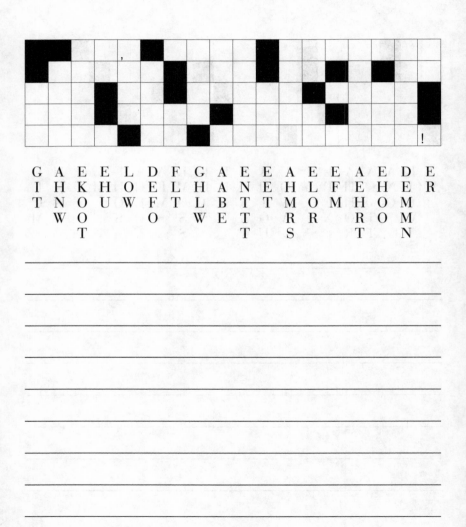

LINE-UP

1 Kings

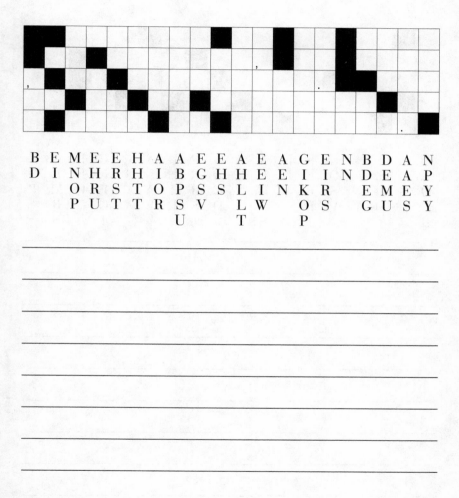

LINE-UP

2 Chronicles

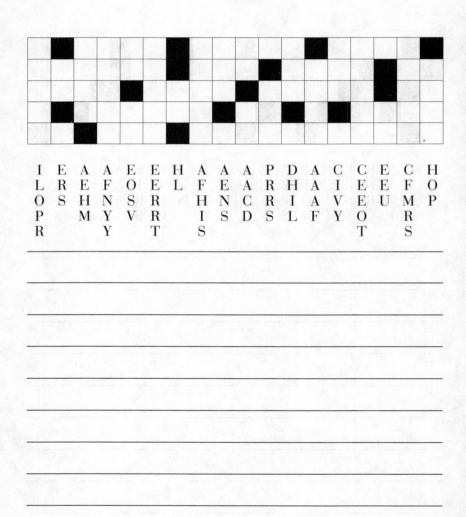

LINE - UP

Job

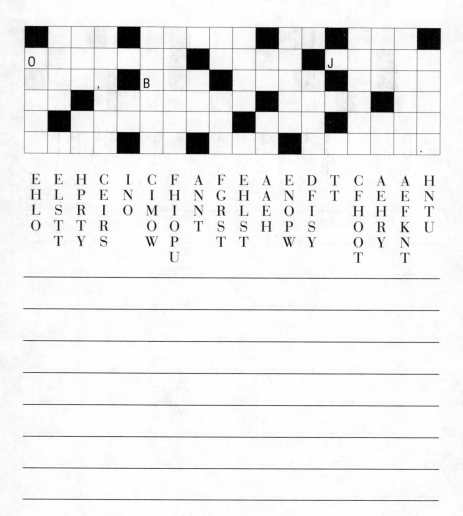

LINE - UP

Isaiah

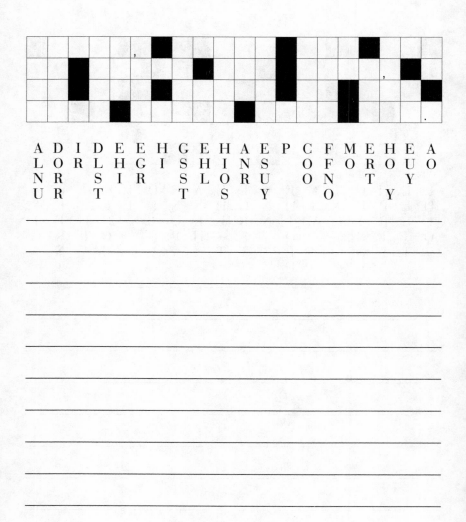

LINE-UP

Luke

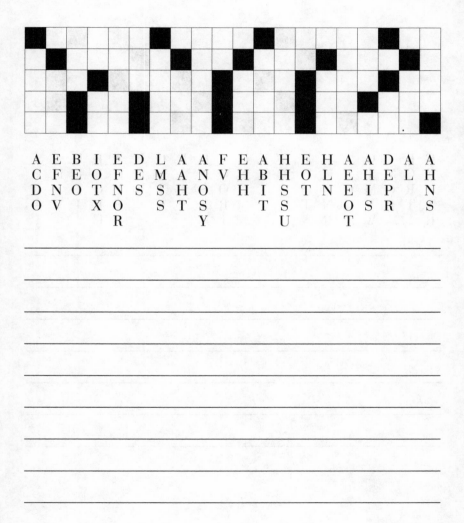

A	E	B	I	E	D	L	A	A	F	E	A	H	E	H	H	A	A	D	A	A
C	F	E	O	F	E	M	A	N	V	H	B	H	O	L	E	E	H	E	L	H
D	N	O	T	N	S	A	S	H	O	I	I	O	L	N	E	H	E	I	P	N
O	V	T	X	O		S	H	O	S	H	S	S	E	E	O	I	P	R	N
				R		S	T	S	Y		T		U		T	O		S		S

LINE-UP

1 Timothy

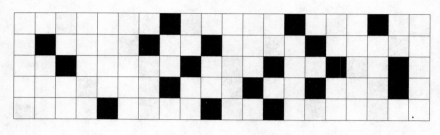

C E I G A H D D E H I H E O E A B E A A
E O M I A H L I N N O N I S O H L E H E
H R O M C N O N O O S I T O P O T S R
N T R R N T P N R T T W P R T T
R W R T R U

_____

_____

_____

_____

_____

_____

230

LINE - UP

2 John

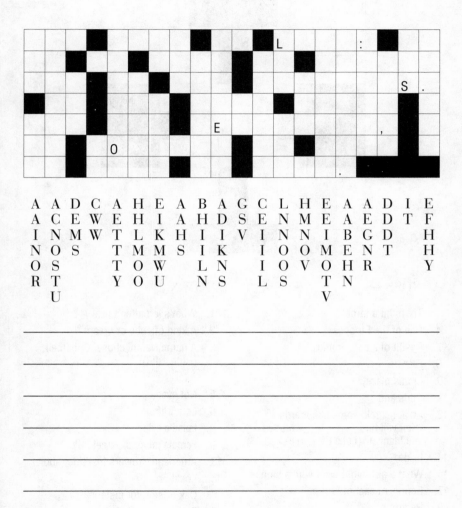

CROSSWORDS

Three Women

ACROSS

1. Try to hit a target
4. One of the Stooges
7. Result of a bad wound
9. Fathers
10. In this place
11. Odds and ____
12. An angel told some shepherds: "You will find ____ ____ wrapped in a blanket" (Luke 2:12, TLB).
14. Pride
15. What a girl might wear with a blouse
17. Continent east of Europe
19. Region
22. The woman who married Boaz
23. Foot part
24. Letter after 6-Down
25. Letter between kay and em

DOWN

1. What's left after a fire
2. A kind of cube or cream
3. A name Naomi chose for herself (Ruth 1:20)
4. A lot
5. Not even
6. Letter after ar
8. Isaac's bride
9. Female judge of Israel
13. American Growers Institute (abbr.)
15. Location
16. Oak or elm, for instance
17. Drawing or painting
18. Take to court
20. Shocking sea creature
21. Everything

CROSSWORDS

Bible Books

ACROSS

1. Book before Psalms
4. Chief petty officer (abbr.)
7. Send out
9. Book before Luke
10. Stream in the desert
11. Book before Obadiah
12. ____ control
14. Frequently, to poets
15. Make you want to scratch
18. Book after Judges
20. Consumes
22. ____-dokey
23. Sweater or jacket
24. Not a Rep. or Ind.
25. Pigpen

DOWN

1. Israelite
2. Actor Sharif
3. ____ one's time
4. Arrived
5. Not an amateur
6. Gives approval to
8. Two NT letters are named for him
9. First book of NT
13. No sharps or flats: the key ____ ____
15. Thing on a list
16. Dumbo's let him fly
17. ERA or RBI
18. Race car: hot ____
19. Hawaiian string instrument, for short
21. Secret agent

CROSSWORDS

Quotes

ACROSS

1. Assist in a crime
5. "I am the ____ for the sheep" (John 10:7, TLB).
9. What a frosh becomes
10. Cheers for a bullfighter
11. Ballet bend
12. Payments to be in a club
13. Boasts
15. Takes too many drugs (abbr.)
16. "____ ____ have sinned, and come short of the glory of God" (Rom. 3:23, KJV).
19. Fold
20. Horse food
23. Half (prefix)
24. Small jar
25. Summer drinks
26. Nervous

DOWN

1. Snake
2. Basketball player Manute
3. Great story
4. "____ ____ ____ my shepherd" (Ps. 23:1, KJV).
5. Lovely quote from 1 John 4:8 (3 wds.)
6. Grad, for short
7. Golf helps
8. Curve
14. Organization for your dentist (abbr.)
16. Give food
17. It's ____ ____: I will pay
18. Placed
19. Boy Scouts of America (abbr.)
21. Game of touching others
22. Wily

STAIRWAYS

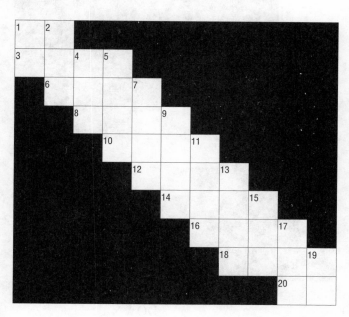

ACROSS

1. Fashionable
3. "Sing a new ____ to the Lord!" (Ps. 96:1, TLB).
6. "Thy ____ is a lamp unto my feet" (Ps. 119:105, KJV).
8. Ripped
10. Cry out loud
12. An ink stain
14. "Deliver us from ____" (Matt. 6:13, KJV).
16. Adam and Eve's home
18. Self-images
20. "Work hard and cheerfully at all you ____" (Col. 3:23, TLB).

DOWN

1. "God ____ love" (1 John 4:8, TLB).
2. "____ is the accepted time" (2 Cor. 6:2, KJV).
4. "Thou shalt ____ steal" (Exod. 20:15, KJV).
5. "God is important because he is the one who makes things ____" (1 Cor. 3:7, TLB).
7. Unexciting
9. Pharaoh's river
11. "I am giving a new commandment to you now—____ each other" (John 13:34, TLB).
13. Ocean movement
15. Table prop
17. Indicate agreement
19. Thus

STAIRWAYS

2

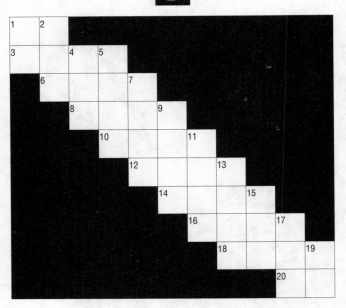

ACROSS

1. A light-switch position
3. "____ not, for I am with you" (Isa. 41:10, TLB).
6. Snare
8. Where Zacchaeus climbed
10. Jacob's bro
12. What's it gonna be: Yes ____ ____?
14. Wise men's guide
16. *Milo and ____:* Animal film
18. Owl sound
20. "So there is now ____ condemnation awaiting those who belong to Christ Jesus" (Rom. 8:1, TLB).

DOWN

1. "Truly this was the Son ____ God" (Matt. 27:54, KJV).
2. Working gear for Peter and Andrew
4. Garfunkel or Linkletter
5. Odd
7. Mexican moola
9. Hearing aids
11. Do ____ others as you would have them . . . (Golden Rule)
13. Vow
15. ____ de Janeiro
17. "This is my beloved ____, and I am wonderfully pleased with him" (Matt. 3:17, TLB).
19. In the direction of

STAIRWAYS

3

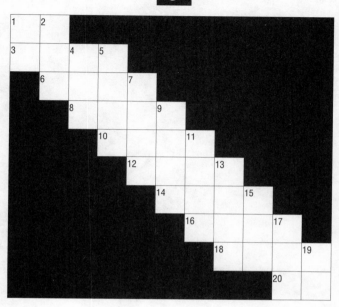

ACROSS

1. "_____ ye doers of the word, and not hearers only" (James 1:22, KJV).
3. "The _____ King Uzziah died I saw the Lord!" (Isa. 6:1, TLB).
6. Fibs
8. Where skating occurs
10. "There is _____ righteous, no, not one" (Rom. 3:10, KJV).
12. Candle part
14. At that time
16. Sign on a shop window
18. Abound
20. "Master, to whom shall _____ go?" (John 6:68, TLB).

DOWN

1. "If we are living now _____ the Holy Spirit's power, let us follow the Holy Spirit's leading" (Gal. 5:25, TLB).
2. Slimy beast
4. Atmosphere
5. Horse controller
7. "I can . . . make you as clean as freshly fallen _____" (Isa. 1:18, TLB).
9. "You . . . _____ [my body] together in my mother's womb" (Ps. 139:13, TLB).
11. Resound
13. "Mary _____ all these things, and pondered them in her heart" (Luke 2:19, KJV).
15. Term for maiden name
17. "And who would use old wineskins to store _____ wine?" (Matt. 9:17, TLB).
19. "Come to _____ and I will give you rest" (Matt. 11:28, TLB).

Section 3

drawing & coloring

COLORING

Joseph and His Coat of Many Colors

Here are a few pictures of people from the Bible. Can you color them in without going outside of the lines?

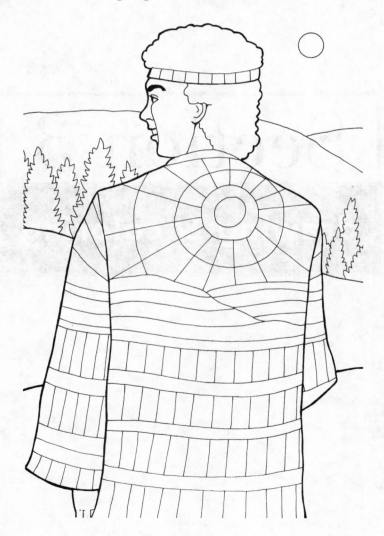

COLORING

Ruth and Boaz

COLORING

Daniel in the Lions' Den

COLORING

Zacchaeus in a Tree

COLORING

Sleepy Eutychus

CONNECT THE DOTS

The Serpent and Eve

Here are pictures of things that happened in the Bible that you need to complete. After you have connected the dots, you can color the pictures.

CONNECT THE DOTS

Jonah and the Great Fish

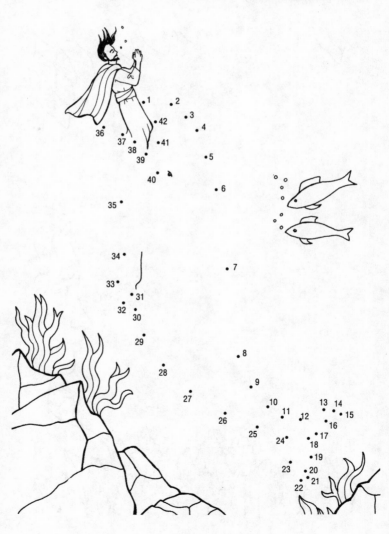

CONNECT THE DOTS

A Wise Man on His Camel

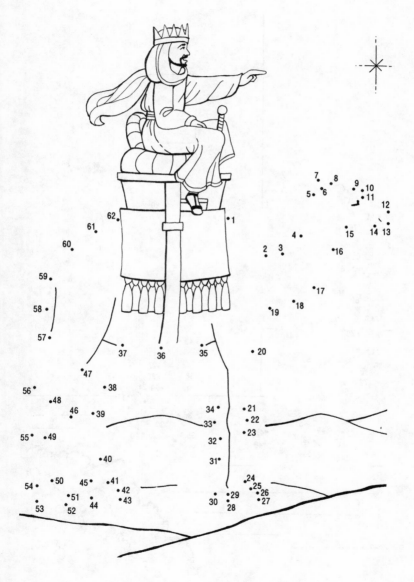

The Donkey That Jesus Rode into Jerusalem

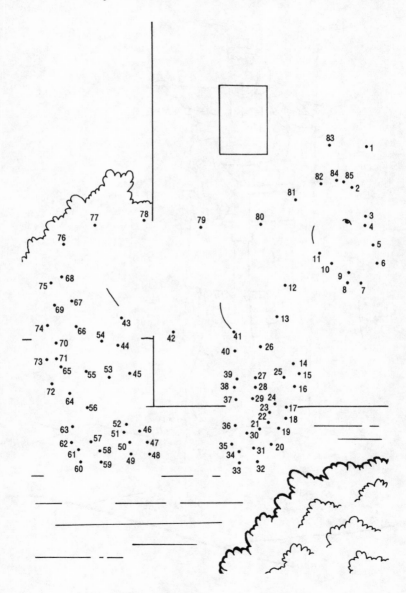

CONNECT THE DOTS

The Rooster That Crowed When Peter Denied Jesus

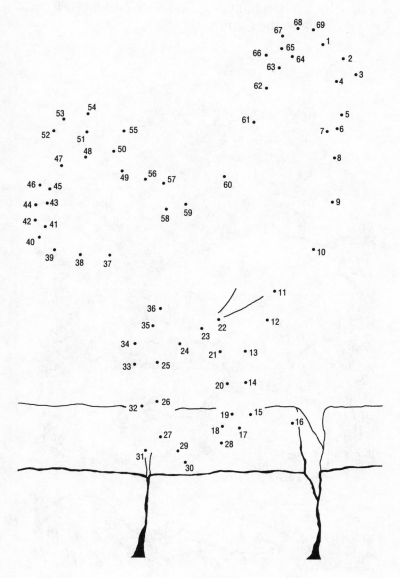

SEARCH AND FIND

The Wilderness

Can you find Moses' staff hidden among the trees and rocks?
When you do, color in the picture.

SEARCH AND FIND

A Lost Sheep

Can you find the lost sheep? When you do, color in the picture.

FILL-INS

Noah's Ark

In each of the following pictures, things have been left out. It's up to you to draw what's missing. When you've finished drawing, color in everything.

What animals are going into the ark? Draw them so Noah can get inside before it starts to rain.

FILL-INS

David, the Shepherd Boy

David played an instrument for his own enjoyment and for King Saul. Draw in his instrument.

FILL-INS

Visiting Baby Jesus

Wise men came to give presents to Jesus when he was a baby. Here is one of the wise men. Suppose you were there to give Jesus a present. Draw yourself and your gift.

Feeding Many People with One Lunch

In one of Jesus' most famous miracles, he turned one boy's lunch into enough food for 5,000 men, plus women and kids. Draw in the food the boy gave Jesus.

John's Vision

When he was an old man, the apostle John had a vision of the future. That vision is written down in the book of Revelation in the Bible. In his vision, John saw some incredible things and creatures. Draw in one or some of those things here in the clouds.

Answers

ANSWERS

■

Part One: Family Fun

MULTIPLE CHOICE (pp. 5–14)

#1 Goin' Down to da Feet
1. **b.** It was holy ground.
2. **b.** Perfume
3. **c.** Peter, but Jesus did anyway.
4. **d.** footstool
5. **d.** All things
6. **a.** blood
7. **d.** John the Baptist (Matt. 3:11)
8. **d.** Iron and clay
9. **b.** He had been lame but had just been healed.
10. **d.** Those who bring good news

#2 Just Kidding (Sons and Daughters)
1. **a.** Jacob (Gen. 34:1)
2. **b.** Peter (Matt. 8:14-15)
3. **d.** John the Baptist (Luke 1:5-25); Zechariah's voice was taken away temporarily because he doubted the angel's message.
4. **b.** Jacob (Gen. 25:24-30); Esau was nicknamed Edom.
5. **c.** Barnabas
6. **b.** Miriam, Moses, and Aaron (Exod. 6:20; 1 Chron. 6:3)
7. **b.** Abraham (Gen. 16)
8. **c.** a son is given
9. **c.** Orpah and Ruth (Ruth 1:3-4)
10. **a.** Peter; this was his Pentecost sermon, when all the disciples were "prophesying" (Acts 2).

#3 Pigging Out
1. **b.** The Corinthians (1 Cor. 11:17-22)
2. **a.** He did, and the pigs ran down the hill into the sea.
3. **c.** The 5,000 Jesus fed with five loaves and two fish (John 6:13)
4. **c.** The Prodigal Son (Luke 15:16)
5. **c.** Their stomach
6. **c.** Pearls (Matt. 7:6)
7. **b.** work . . . eat

8. **a.** Peter (Acts 10:11-13); God was about to ask him to preach to "unclean" Gentiles.
9. **d.** Jesus
10. **b.** Ezekiel (Ezek. 3:1-3), who did a lot of odd things

#4 Fast Forward
1. **a.** The shepherds (Luke 2:16)
2. **c.** The sun
3. **d.** Esau (Gen. 25:30)
4. **a.** His thousand wives and concubines
5. **b.** A fool
6. **d.** The prophet Jonah (Jon. 3:5; 4:1), who apparently wanted them to suffer for their wickedness
7. **b.** Daniel, or **d.** Shadrach (Dan. 1:4-7); Meshach or Abednego would also be acceptable.
8. **b.** Jonathan's father (King Saul) was trying to kill David (1 Sam. 20:33-38).
9. **d.** An angel (Acts 12:7), who released Peter from prison
10. **c.** Lot (Gen. 19:15), before his escape from Sodom

#5 Give Me a Hand
1. **d.** Revelation (Rev. 1:16); Jesus was holding the stars.
2. **b.** Abraham (Gen. 22:12), after nearly sacrificing Isaac
3. **b.** Jacob (Gen. 25:26)
4. **c.** Thomas (John 20:25), speaking of Jesus, of course
5. **c.** A cloud (1 Kings 18:44)
6. **c.** Daniel (Dan. 5)
7. **a.** What your right hand is doing
8. **d.** Judas; Jesus said that the one who dipped his hand in the bowl with him would betray him.
9. **a.** He did this on the day of rest.
10. **d.** The wall of Jerusalem

ANSWERS

#6 Red All Over
1. **c.** Esau (Gen. 25:30)
2. **d.** Jesus (Matt. 27:28-29)
3. **c.** Miriam (Exod. 15:20)
4. **a.** Black and white
5. **b.** The Israelites' tabernacle (Exod. 26:14)
6. **c.** Song of Songs (Song 4:3)
7. **d.** Rahab (Josh. 2:21)
8. **a.** as white as snow
9. **c.** "A wife of noble character"
10. **c.** Job (Job 16:16-17)

#7 Big and Little
1. **c.** Five small bread loaves, which Jesus multiplied to feed 5,000
2. **b.** Saul (1 Sam. 9:2)
3. **a.** Climbed a tree (Luke 19:1-10)
4. **c.** The Sea of Galilee (or Sea of Tiberias) (John 21:1-14)
5. **c.** Jesus, in the Sermon on the Mount (Matt. 5:18)
6. **c.** Absalom (2 Sam. 18:9)
7. **b.** Samuel's mother Hannah (1 Sam. 2:19); the boy was being raised by the tabernacle priest, and she visited him once a year.
8. **c.** Goliath (1 Sam. 17:4-7)
9. **a.** The tongue (James 3:4-5)
10. **d.** Jonah (Jon. 1:17)

#8 Grounds for Action
1. **d.** Gideon (Judg. 6:36-38); he asked that the ground be dew-covered and the fleece dry, then vice versa.
2. **b.** His staff (Exod. 4:3)
3. **b.** Birds, precisely sparrows
4. **a.** The Red Sea (Exod. 14:29), or **b.** The Jordan River (Josh. 3:17)
5. **a.** Saul, also known as Paul (Acts 9:1-4), at his miraculous conversion
6. **d.** The soldiers who came to arrest Jesus (John 18:6)
7. **b.** In a third-story window; Paul healed him.
8. **b.** Noah (Gen. 8:13)
9. **a.** Goliath (1 Sam. 17:49)

10. **c.** Moses and Elijah (Matt. 17:1-13), at the Mount of Transfiguration

#9 Kings and Queens
1. **d.** Melchizedek (Gen. 14:18-20)
2. **b.** Jezebel (1 Kings 19:1-2)
3. **c.** Hezekiah (2 Kings 20:1-11)
4. **c.** Herod Agrippa (Acts 26:28)
5. **a.** Solomon (1 Kings 10:1-13)
6. **b.** Nebuchadnezzar (Dan. 2)
7. **d.** There would be seven years of plenty, followed by seven years of famine (Gen. 41:1-40).
8. **d.** Esther (Esther 2:1-18)
9. **b.** Athaliah (2 Kings 11:1-3)
10. **b.** David (1 Chron. 28)

#10 Hear! Hear!
1. **b.** A man who builds his house on the sand (Matt. 7:24-27)
2. **a.** A servant named Malchus (Luke 22:50-51; John 18:10)
3. **c.** Sarah (Gen. 18:12); the baby's name, Isaac, meant "laughter."
4. **d.** Paul's nephew (Acts 23:16); he warned the soldiers and saved Paul.
5. **b.** Samuel (1 Sam. 3)
6. **a.** Abel's (Gen. 4:10), the first murder victim
7. **b.** Jacob (Gen. 42:2); little did he know that his son Joseph was running things in Egypt.
8. **c.** Moses (Exod. 3:7)
9. **c.** Nehemiah (Neh. 1:4), who then returned to Jerusalem to oversee construction of the wall
10. **a.** The queen of Sheba (1 Kings 10:1)

CATEGORIES (pp. 15–20)
#1 Pyramid
1. People (things) who dealt with fish
2. Books of the Bible named for people
3. People with double letters in their names
4. People who were healed
5. People who traveled to Egypt
6. Names that end in *b*

ANSWERS

7. People who built altars
8. People who gave gifts
9. People who met with kings
10. Shepherds

#2 Do-It-Yourself Pyramid
There are no lists for giving clues. Any clues are fine, as long as they are correct and lead the others toward the right answer.

#3 "Feud"
1. List a miracle Jesus did. (100 points total)
   Turned water into wine 46
   Fed 5,000/loaves & fishes 24
   Raised Lazarus 13
   Healed lame/blind/lepers 9
   Walked on water 8
2. Name an author of a book of the Bible. (100 points total)
   Paul 51
   John 18
   Moses 12
   Luke 9
   James 5
   Matthew 5
3. Name a Bible character who lied. (100 points total)
   Ananias/Sapphira 39
   Peter 23
   Cain 11
   Judas 11
   Delilah 8
   Jacob 8
4. Name a city or town mentioned in the Bible. (100 points total)
   Jerusalem 39
   Bethlehem 33
   Sodom 9
   Jericho 7
   Capernaum 6
   Nazareth 6
5. Name two back-to-back books of the Bible. (100 points total)
   Matthew-Mark 42
   Genesis-Exodus 35

1 & 2 Corinthians 9
Psalms-Proverbs 8
Acts-Romans 6
6. Name a king mentioned in the Bible. (100 points total)
   David 40
   Herod 17
   Solomon 13
   Saul 9
   Hezekiah 8
   Nebuchadnezzar 8
   Ahab 5
7. Name an animal mentioned in the Bible. (100 points total)
   Donkey 36
   Sheep/lamb 24
   Lion 21
   Snake/serpent 7
   Cattle/oxen 6
   Horse 6
8. List a time in the Bible when people sang. (100 points total)
   Exodus/Red Sea crossing 35
   Palm Sunday/Triumphal Entry 12
   When David brought the ark into Jerusalem 12
   After winning battles 8
   Feasts/holy days 8
   When Paul & Silas were in prison 5
   Around the golden calf 4
   Mary's song (The Magnificat) 4
   On the way to worship in the temple 4
   The dedication of the temple in Jerusalem 4
   When Nehemiah rebuilt the Jerusalem wall 4
9. List something that David did. (100 points total)
   Killed Goliath 54
   Committed adultery with Bathsheba 18
   Played the harp 9
   Danced before the Lord 8
   Wrote the Psalms 6
   Killed a bear and/or lion while shepherding 5

ANSWERS

10. List something that Moses did.
    (100 points total)
    Parted Red Sea 41
    Received Ten Commandments 22
    Led Israelites out of Egypt 14
    Smashed the Ten Commandments 8
    Hit a rock to get water 6
    Confronted Pharaoh 5
    Met God at the burning bush 4

11. Name a tribe of Israel. (100 points
    total)
    Judah 45
    Benjamin 23
    Levi 22
    Dan 10

12. Name a town that Paul visited.
    (100 points total)
    Rome 27
    Corinth 26
    Ephesus 24
    Philippi 11
    Antioch 7
    Damascus 5

STEP QUIZZES (pp. 22–52)

#1 People
A. Eve (Gen. 2:21-22; 3:4, 20; 4:1;
   2 Cor. 11:3)
B. Jacob (Gen. 27; 32:28; 35:22; 37:3;
   47:9)
C. Jonah (Jon. 2:1, 5, 10; 3:4-5)
D. Esther (Esther 2:7, 17; 4:11–5:2;
   7:6)
E. Joshua (Exod. 24:13; Num. 11:28;
   Josh. 6; 10:12-15; 12:1-5)
F. Elisha (2 Kings 2:13-14, 23; 5; 6:1,
   18)
G. John the Baptist (Matt. 3:15; 14:10;
   Luke 1:57-64; John 1:20)
H. Noah (Gen. 5:25-28; 6:10, 15; 7:2;
   8:6-9)
I. Isaac (Gen. 22:1-12; 24:29, 67;
   25:24-26; 27; 35:25-26; Rom. 9:7)
J. Peter (Matt. 16:16, 23; 26:73; Acts
   2:15; 5:29)

#2 People
A. Matthew (Levi) (Matt. 2; 9:9-13;
   10:2-4)
B. Cain (Gen. 2:15; 4:2-15)
C. Samson (Judg. 14–16)
D. Rachel (Gen. 29:9-10, 18-28; 31:34;
   35:16-20, 24)
E. Moses (Exod. 2:21; 3:1; 5:1;
   17:10-13; 24:15-18)
F. Thomas (John 11:16; 14:6; 20:24-25)
G. The Pharisees (Matt. 22:35-36;
   23:16, 24; John 9:17; Phil. 3:5); you
   can accept "scribes" or even
   "lawyers" for level 1.
H. David (1 Sam. 16:10-13; 17:48-51;
   21:12-15; 24:4; 2 Sam. 15:13)
I. Jesus (Matt. 1:22-25; 3:17; 8:28-34;
   17:17; 27:35)
J. Methuselah (Gen. 5:21-27)

#3 People
A. Saul (1 Sam. 10; 18:20; 24:4;
   28:7-8)
B. Martha (Luke 10:40; John 11:1-2,
   21, 39)
C. Solomon (1 Kings 1:39; 3:5, 25;
   6:37; 9:15)
D. Abraham (Gen. 11:26; 12:5; 15:5;
   18:12; 22:10-11)
E. Paul (Acts 9:5, 17-18, 25; 16:9;
   22:21)
F. James and John (Matt. 4:21; 20:21;
   26:36-40; Mark 3:16-19)
G. Delilah (Judg. 16)
H. Gideon (Judg. 6:32; 7:5-6, 16-22;
   8:22; 9:1)
I. Ruth (Ruth 1–4)
J. Aaron (Exod. 4:14; 7:10; 40:12-13;
   Num. 12:1; Ps. 133:2)

#4 People
A. Job (Job 1–2; 42:13)
B. Barnabas (Acts 4:36; 11:25; 13–14;
   15:39)
C. Paul (Acts 7:58; 9:1-9; 17:6; 28:1-6)
D. Judas Iscariot (Matt. 26:15; 27:5;
   John 12:5; Acts 1:26)

E. Timothy (Acts 16:2; 1 Cor. 4:16-17; 2 Tim. 1:5; 2:15)

F. Goliath (1 Sam. 17)

G. Noah (Gen. 6:9, 12-13; 7:6; 9:9-17; Matt. 24:37)

H. Isaac (Gen. 18:9-14; 21:1-3; 25:24-30; 26:20-22; 27:46)

I. David (1 Sam. 17:35-36; 2 Sam. 6:14; 11:26-27; 16:5-14; 18:33)

J. Pontius Pilate (Matt. 27:2, 15, 26; John 19:12, 22)

#5 People

A. Elisha (2 Kings 2:9, 15; 5:10; 9:1-3; 13:14)

B. Solomon (1 Kings 3:12; 10:7; 11:43; Prov. 1:7; Matt. 6:29)

C. John the Baptist (Matt. 3:3-4; 14:1-8; Luke 1:20)

D. Samson (Judg. 13:2; 15:14, 16; 16:4, 21-22)

E. Abraham, or Abram (Gen. 14:18-20; 18:22-33; 21:1-5; 24:1-10)

F. The Pharisees (Matthew 12:8, 24; 23:27-28; Luke 18:9-14; 19:37-40)

G. Gideon (Judg. 6:25-28, 36-40; 7:16-22; 8:1-3, 21)

H. Jacob (Gen. 25:24-34; 30:21)

I. Jonah (Jon. 1:11-17; 3:4-10; 4:1, 6)

J. Job (Job 1–2; 32:2-4; 40:15)

#6 People

A. Jesus (Matt. 2:1; 15:32-38; Mark 9:50; Luke 2:25-38; John 20:15)

B. John (John 13:23; 19:26-27; 20:3-4; 2 John 1; 3 John 1; Rev. 1:11)

C. Saul (1 Sam. 9:2-9; 18:1-12; 31:3-4)

D. Peter (Matt. 16:18; Mark 14:29-31; John 1:40; 6:68; 21:15)

E. Pharaoh, king of Egypt (Gen. 41:17-21; Exod. 5:1; 8:18-19; 14:28; Isa. 30:2-3) [The question refers to the role of pharaoh, king of Egypt, not to any particular man. Obviously, these Scriptures speak of several different rulers in different times.]

F. Timothy (2 Cor. 1:1; Phil. 1:1; 1 Tim. 6:10; 2 Tim. 2:3-4; 3:15; 4:13)

G. Moses (Exod. 2:9-10; 3:2; 6:20)

H. John the Baptist (Matt. 3:4, 7, 11; Luke 1:63; 7:28)

I. Samson (Judg. 14:15-20; 15:15; 16:6-15, 26)

J. Abraham, or Abram (Gen. 11:26, 29; 16:15; 22:2; Rom. 4:3)

#7 People

A. Peter (Matt. 14:29; 16:22; 17:26-27; John 13:9; Acts 1:21)

B. Ezekiel (Ezek. 2:1; 4:4-5; 5:1; 10; 37:1-2)

C. Jesus (Matt. 2:11; John 21:13; Phil. 2:6; Heb. 5:6; Rev. 22:16)

D. Saul (1 Sam. 10:26; 13:8-14; 15; 17:38-39)

E. Jonah (Jon. 1:2-3, 17; 2:10; Matt. 12:39-40)

F. Jacob (Gen. 29:18, 23-28; 32:26; 35:23)

G. Abraham, or Abram (Gen. 12; 13:12; 17:2-4; 20; 25:9)

H. John the Baptist (Matt. 3:13-14; 9:14; 11:14; Luke 3:11; John 1:29)

I. Joseph (Gen. 30:1-24; 35:24; 37:21-22; 39:1; 41:37-44; 50:2)

J. Judas Iscariot (Matt. 26:47, 50; 27:7; Luke 22:47-48; John 12:6)

#8 People

A. Luke (Luke 1:1; 2:8-20; Acts 1:1; Col. 4:14; 2 Tim. 4:11)

B. Jacob (Gen. 27:15; 28:12; 30:31-43; 32:22-25; 35:22-26)

C. Peter (Matt. 18:21; John 13:6-10; 20:6-7; 21:3; Acts 4:12)

D. Nehemiah (Neh. 1:11; 2:4, 10; 4:16; 5:14)

E. Isaiah (Isa. 6:1-4, 6-7; 8:3; 9:6)

F. Jesse (1 Sam. 16; Matt. 1:5)

G. Ishmael (Gen. 16:9-12, 15; 17:20; 21:9; 25:9)

H. Miriam (Exod. 15:20; Num. 12:1, 9-15; 20:1)

ANSWERS

―

I. Pontius Pilate (Matt. 27:11, 19, 24; John 18:36; 19:19-20)

J. Lazarus (John 11:1-2, 11, 17, 43; 12:10-11)

#9 People

A. Jesus (Matt. 3:13-14; 14:25-32; Luke 19:5; 23:30; John 8:6)

B. Stephen (Acts 6:5, 9-10; 7:54-60)

C. Benjamin (Gen. 35:24; 42:32; 44:1-6; Judg. 20:46-47; 1 Sam. 9:1-2; Phil. 3:5)

D. Rebekah (Gen. 24:18-19, 62-64; 25:24-28; 27:42; 35:25)

E. Herod (Matt. 2:1-16)

F. Apollos (Acts 18:24–19:1; 1 Cor. 3:6)

G. Solomon (1 Kings 2; 3:12; 11:3; 12; Song of Sol. 1:2)

H. Ahab (1 Kings 16:30-31; 17:1; 21:19; 22:8)

I. Andrew (Mark 1:16; John 1:40-41; 6:8-9; 12:22)

J. Nicodemus (John 3:1-4; 19:39)

#10 People

A. Hagar (Gen. 16:1-9, 15; Gal. 4:24-25)

B. Joseph of Arimathea (Matt. 27:57-60; Luke 23:50-52; John 19:38-40)

C. Rachel (Gen. 29:16-17, 29; 30:1; Jer. 31:15)

D. Malachi (Mal. 1:1; 3:8; 4:2, 5)

E. Balaam (Num. 22; 2 Pet. 2:15; Jude 11)

F. Absalom (2 Sam. 15:13, 32-34; 18:6-17)

G. Laban (Gen. 29:16, 22-27; 30:31-34; 31:45-53; 35:24)

H. Philip (Acts 6:5; 8:5-8, 13, 27, 36)

I. Peter (Matt. 8:14-15; John 1:42; 18:11; Acts 9:36-41; 12:6-11)

J. Belshazzar (Dan. 5)

#11 Places

A. Jerusalem (Ps. 137:5; Luke 2:41-50; 13:4; 21:20-24; John 19:17)

B. Bethlehem (Ruth 1:22; 4:1-13; Matt. 2:16; Luke 2:1-7)

C. The Sea of Galilee (Matt. 15:29-38; Mark 1:16-18; 4:39; John 6:1, 16-21)

D. Mount Sinai, or Mount Horeb (Exod. 3:1; 20:1-17; 1 Kings 19:8; Acts 7:38; Gal. 4:24-25)

E. Egypt (Gen. 12:15; 49:33; Exod. 8:1, 6; 2 Kings 23:29)

F. Ephesus (Acts 19:15, 23-41; 20:28; Eph. 6:11; 1 Tim. 1:3)

G. Mount Ararat (Gen. 8:3-4, 8-12; 9:1; 2 Kings 19:37)

H. Athens (Acts 17:18-28)

I. The temple in Jerusalem (1 Kings 5:13-17; 2 Kings 11:3; Jer. 7:11; Ezek. 40–42; Acts 21:26-28)

J. Jericho (Josh. 6:2-4, 26; Mark 10:46-49; Luke 10:30; 19:8)

#12 Places

A. Babylon (Ps. 137; Isa. 14:23; Jer. 25:11; Dan. 2:49; 5:26-28)

B. Jericho (Josh. 2:1, 6; 6:20; 7:1; 2 Kings 2:15)

C. The Garden of Eden (Gen. 2–3)

D. Jordan River (Josh. 3:9-17; 2 Kings 2:8; 5:10; 6:6; Matt. 3:13-17)

E. Rome (Acts 22:27; Rom. 6:23; 15:24; 16:13; Phil. 4:22)

F. Nineveh (Jon. 2–3; 4:11; Nah. 1:1)

G. The Red Sea (Exod. 14:15, 22, 28; 15:1, 20)

H. Nazareth (Luke 1:26-27; 2:51-52; 4:22, 28-30; John 1:46)

I. Babel, Tower of (Gen. 11:1-9; Acts 2:4-6)

J. Garden of Gethsemane (Matt. 26:36-40; Mark 14:43; Luke 22:50-51; John 18:2, 10)

#13 Places

A. Bethlehem (1 Sam. 16:1, 7; 2 Sam. 23:14-17; Mic. 5:2; Matt. 2:8)

B. Bethany (Matt. 26:6-7; Mark 11:12-14; John 11:35; 12:1-2, 9)

ANSWERS

C. Egypt (Gen. 16:1; 46:28; Exod. 12; Num. 11:4-5; Jer. 43:6)

D. Capernaum (Matt. 4:12-13; 8:5, 14-15; 11:23-24; Mark 2:1-4; John 6:16-21)

E. Jerusalem (Judg. 19:10; 1 Kings 10:27; Ps. 122:6; Matt. 5:35; Acts 1:4)

F. Sodom (Gen. 14:11-12, 16; 19:17, 26)

G. Samaria (Ezek. 16:46; Luke 9:52-55; John 4:9, 20; Acts 8:18) [The name Samaria was used for both a city, the capital of the Northern Kingdom, and the surrounding region.]

H. Mount Sinai (Exod. 24:18; 32:2-3, 14-15; Deut. 1:1-5; 1 Kings 19:12-13)

I. Damascus (2 Kings 5:12; 16:10; Acts 9:1-18, 25)

J. The temple in Jerusalem (2 Sam. 7:5; Ezra 6:15; Mark 15:38; Luke 21:2; Acts 3:1-8)

#14 Things, etc.

A. Loaves and fishes (Luke 9:12-17; John 6:2-15)

B. Moses' rod (Exod. 4:2-3; 14:21; 17:1-7, 11-13; Num. 20:11)

C. The tree of conscience, or the tree of the knowledge of good and evil (Gen. 2:16-17; 3:1-6)

D. Joseph's colored coat (Gen. 37:3-4, 23, 28, 31-35)

E. Honey (Num. 13:27; Judg. 14:14, 18; Ps. 19:10; Matt. 3:4; Rev. 10:9-10)

F. The manger (Luke 2:7, 10-12)

G. David's slingshot (1 Sam. 17:40-49)

H. Coins, or "pennies" (Matt. 17:26-27; Mark 12:14-16; Luke 15:8-9; 21:2)

I. Golden calf (Exod. 32:1-4, 19-20, 24)

J. Noah's ark, or boat (Gen. 6:14-15; 7:5-24; 8:3-4)

#15 Things, etc.

A. The serpent, or snake (Gen. 3:1-5, 14-15)

B. Samson's hair (Judg. 16:13-21)

C. Chariot of fire (2 Kings 2:11-12)

D. The cross (Mark 15:46; Luke 23:26; John 19:20; Gal. 6:14; Col. 2:14)

E. Fig tree (Matt. 21:19; John 1:48; James 3:12)

F. Aaron's rod (Exod. 7:10-12; 8:16-17; Num. 17:1-11)

G. Manna (Exod. 16:15, 31; Num. 11:8; Ps. 78:23-25)

H. The great fish, or whale (Jon. 1–2; Matt. 12:39-40)

I. Donkey, or donkey's colt (Zech. 9:9; Matt. 21:1-9; Luke 19:30-34; John 12:13)

J. Stone tablets (Exod. 32:16, 19; 34:1-2, 28)

#16 Things, etc.

A. Flaming, or fiery, furnace (Dan. 3)

B. A fleece (Judg. 6:36-40)

C. Cloud, or bright cloud, or pillar of fire (Exod. 13:21; 24:15-18; 40:34-38; Matt. 17:5)

D. The handwriting on the wall (Dan. 5:5-8, 24-31)

E. Plow, or plowshares (1 Kings 19:19, 21; Mic. 4:3; Joel 3:10)

F. Axhead (2 Kings 6:1-7)

G. Ark of the covenant, or ark of the Lord (Exod. 25:10, 18; 37:1; 1 Sam. 5:1-3; 2 Sam. 6:14-15)

H. Wings (Isa. 6:2; 40:31; Mal. 4:2; Matt. 23:37; Rev. 9:9)

I. The walls of Jerusalem (Neh. 4:3; 6:15; Isa. 36:13; Jer. 52:14; Rev. 21:16-17)

J. Gold, frankincense, and myrrh (Matt. 2:11-12)

ANSWERS

LOGIC PROBLEMS (54–75)

Animals

The two pets that aren't four-legged are the snake and the raven. Since Moses has one (#3) and it can't be the snake (since he started with that), Moses must now have the raven and Balaam the snake. The only two owners whose names begin with the same letter (#4) are David and Daniel—so they must have the lion and lamb. David started with the lamb, so he now has the lion, and Daniel must have the lamb. That leaves Elijah with the donkey, named Hank (#2). The lamb and snake must be named Buddy and Brenda (#1), but Buddy's owner's name comes first alphabetically (#7), so he must be the snake that belongs to Balaam, and Brenda is Daniel's lamb. Since Roger is not the raven (#9), he must be the lion. And the raven is Felicia.

The answer looks like this:
Balaam, snake, Buddy
Daniel, lamb, Brenda
David, lion, Roger
Elijah, donkey, Hank
Moses, raven, Felicia

2 Kings

Miriam couldn't have gone to Bethel or Bethany (#12) or to either of the mountains (#9), so she went to Jezreel. Similarly, Abigail didn't go to a B place (#12) or to Mt. Tabor (#10), so she must have gone to Mt. Gerizim. Simon didn't go to Bethany (#6) or to Mt. Tabor (#3), which leaves Bethel. Marcus didn't go to Mt. Tabor (#9), so he must have gone to Bethany, which leaves Mt. Tabor for Frodo. Abigail must have been the asparagus-provider (#8). And Simon made the hammer fly (#1). The lightning-caller must then be Frodo or Miriam (#4), but it can't be Frodo (#11), so it's Miriam. That leaves Marcus as the M name who invented Alka-Seltzer (#5), and Frodo must have stood on his head.

The answer looks like this:
Simon, Bethel, hammer flying
Marcus, Bethany, Alka-Seltzer
Abigail, Mt. Gerizim, asparagus
Miriam, Jezreel, lightning
Frodo, Mt. Tabor, stood on head

1 Chronicles

Noah is Lamech's son, and since there's only one bass, that's his part. Methusaleh had three great-grandsons— Shem, Ham and Japheth—but Japheth and Ham (Canaan's dad) aren't included, so it must be Shem singing "O Come All Ye Faithful." And he must be a baritone because that song and "Joy to the World" are sung in the same part; there are only two tenors, and one sings "Silent Night." (And by the way, Noah and Shem are one of our father-son combinations.) Judah is the only one listed with 11 brothers and 5 sons, so he sings "Angels We Have Heard." And, by elimination, he must be the other tenor. So who is the tenor who sings "Silent Night" and who is the baritone who sings "Joy"? (By elimination, we can give "Hark the Herald" to Noah, the bass.) Well, Abraham has two grandsons listed, Jacob and Esau, and they are both sons of Isaac, who must be the baritone singing "Joy." But Jacob is also Judah's father. If Jacob is the

ANSWERS

—■—

other tenor, then there are three father-son pairs, and two tenors have their fathers in the group. So it must be Esau singing "Silent Night."

The final arrangement looks like this:
Noah, a bass, sings "Hark the Herald."
Shem, a baritone, sings "O Come All Ye Faithful."
Isaac, a baritone, sings "Joy to the World."
Esau, a tenor, sings "Silent Night."
Judah, a tenor, sings "Angels We Have Heard on High."

Job
Eliphaz wore the raven tattoo (#4). The other bird, the ostrich, must be on Zophar (#7). Eliphaz and Elihu received the oxen and camel (#3), but the camel went to the behemoth-tattoo-wearer (#8)—not Eliphaz—so it must be Eliphaz-oxen-raven and Elihu-behemoth-camel. The gold ring did not go to Zophar (#6) or Job (who received nothing), so it must be Bildad's. That leaves Zophar with the silver piece. Bildad then wore the Leviathan tattoo (#1), which leaves the lion tattoo for Job.

The answer then looks like this:
Job, lion, no gift
Bildad, Leviathan, gold ring
Eliphaz, raven, oxen
Zophar, ostrich, silver piece
Elihu, behemoth, camel

Psalms
Barnabas plays Psalm 103 (#1), so Deborah must play Psalm 119 (#4). Caleb plays Psalm 1 (#5). The only man remaining is Ehud, so he's the one who plays Psalm 19 (#2). That leaves Anna playing Psalm 42. The harpist is a woman who plays a two-digit psalm (#3, #6). That must be Anna on Psalm 42. So Deborah, the other woman, must play the high cymbals (#6). The low-cymbal player must be playing Psalm 1 (#7), so that's Caleb. The trumpeter cannot be Barnabas (#8), so it must be Ehud. That leaves Barnabas as the lyre player.

The answer looks like this:
Anna, harp, 42
Barnabas, lyre, 103
Caleb, low cymbals, 1
Deborah, high cymbals, 119
Ehud, trumpet, 19

Daniel
Let's start with Susa. Clue 1 tells us it was capital to the three-city ruler and clue 5 identifies it with the one who lost his appointment book. Since the broccoli lover was not based in Elam or Media (#10) or Ur (which was home to the okra lover—clue 11), he must be based in Susa. Clue 12 tells us this broccoli-Susa-appointment-book-three-city ruler was not Shadrach or Meshach, which leaves Daniel and Abednego. More on that later.

What do we know about Meshach? Since Shadrach was not based in Susa, clue 9

ANSWERS

---

says Meshach must be from Media. That means he is not the Ur-based okra lover (#11), and he doesn't like broccoli (#12). Since the spinach lover rules four cities (#6) and Meshach cannot rule four cities (#2), then Meshach's vegetable must be lima beans. That means he was nearly strangled by the hanging gardens (#3). Since the three-city ruler is not Meshach (see above), Meshach must rule one or two cities. But the two-city ruler must be the dreamer (#7, with broccoli info above), so Meshach rules one city.

That means Abednego must rule two (#2), which leaves Daniel as the Susa person who rules three. By elimination, it's Shadrach who rules four. Then Shadrach is the spinach lover (#6) and Abednego the okra lover (by elimination). Then Abednego is based in Ur (#11) and Shadrach in Elam (elimination). Abednego, the two-city ruler, is the dreamer, which leaves Shadrach as the one who lost carvings in the fire.

So the answer looks like this:
Shadrach, four cities, Elam, spinach, carvings burnt
Daniel, three cities, Susa, broccoli, lost appointment book
Abednego, two cities, Ur, okra, nervous breakdown
Meshach, one city, Media, lima beans, nearly strangled

Micah
We know the sword gets beaten into the plowshare under the fig tree (#1). The shield did not become the hoe (#3, #4) and was not the back-scratcher (#5), so it must have been beaten into the sickel—under a plum tree (#4). The arrows became back-scratchers (#5), and must not have been under the date tree (#3), so this was under the juniper. That leaves the spear to be beaten into the hoe, under the date tree. Now who did all this? Darla must be the arrow-back-scratcher-juniper person (#2). That leaves the sickel combination for Cyrus (#7). The only consonant left (#8) is B for Benjamin, so he gets the spear-hoe-date combo. That leaves Abel for the biblical sword-plowshare-fig group.

The answer looks like this:
Abel, sword, plowshare, fig tree
Benjamin, spear, hoe, date tree
Cyrus, shield, sickel, plum tree
Darla, arrows, back-scratchers, juniper tree

Zechariah
Clue 1 tells us the "Branch" lamp connects to the gold pipe. Silver and bronze are the other metals in Daniel 2:32, so they must connect with "Son of Man" and "Ancient of Days" (#4). Since silver also leads to a lamp starting with the same letter as tin's lamp (#3), it must be "Son of Man," which leaves bronze with "Ancient of Days" and tin as "Sun of Righteousness." Since silver is now taken, "Ruler" must hook up to the copper pipe (#8). And zinc cannot be "Root" (#7), so it must be "Prince of Peace." That leaves the iron pipe for the "Root" lamp. Two of the three left-side pipes (#2) are copper and zinc (#5). Since zinc connects with "Prince of Peace," the third left pipe must be iron (#6). That leaves silver, tin, bronze, and gold as the right-side pipes.

You know, it feels a bit funny to be playing around with these great names of our Lord. Take a minute to think about them and how they were fulfilled in Jesus.

ANSWERS

The answer looks like this:
Ancient of Days, bronze, right
Branch, gold, right
Prince of Peace, zinc, left
Root, iron, left
Ruler, copper, left
Son of Man, silver, right
Sun of Righteousness, tin, right

Romans
There were two men who received gifts (#2), and only two men, since four women are listed. One of these was Rufus (v. 13; #6). These two men received gifts from Laodicea and Damascus (clue 2). Since Rufus got the eye salve, and the two medicinal gifts came from Laodicea and Philippi (clue 1), his eye salve must be from Laodicea. The other medicinal gift, olive oil, had to come from Philippi. The Philippi gift went to either Persis or Mary (#4; vs. 6,12), but Persis got the cloak (clue 7), so Mary must have the olive oil from Philippi.

That means Priscilla's gift must come from Ephesus (which received the epistle that precedes Philippians, see #8), and that gift was parchment (#5). "All the churches of the Gentiles" were grateful to Priscilla and her husband Aquila (vs. 3, 4). Since Priscilla got the parchment, it must be Aquila who got the camel whip (#3). He must be that second man, and so the whip must have come from Damascus (#2). Phoebe's gift came from Corinth (#9), and it must be the other item of clothing (clue 10), the toga. By elimination, then, the cloak that Persis received was from Colosse.

The answer looks like this:
Phoebe, toga, Corinth
Priscilla, parchment, Ephesus
Aquila, camel whip, Damascus
Rufus, eye salve, Laodicea
Mary, olive oil, Philippi
Persis, cloak, Colosse

Philemon
The singer and pray-er had names beginning with the same letter (#4). Since these are the only two non-reading activities, Archippus must be one of them (#8), and Apphia the other. And since Apphia would not be called "son" (#12), Archippus prayed and Apphia sang. Since Apphia could not be in the purple (#1), brown (#3), white (#5), or scarlet (#10) room, she must be in the gray room. Similarly, Archippus can't be in the purple (#1), white (#5 with #8), or scarlet (#10 with #8) room. So he's in the brown room. Only Philemon or Apphia would call Archippus "son" (#12), and Apphia is spoken for, so it must be Philemon in the white room. Thus he did not read Paul's epistles (#10). And we know he didn't read the Old Testament (#6). So Philemon must have read the Gospels. Since Paul did not read his own epistles (#2), he must have read from the Old Testament. And he's the only remaining P name to stay in the purple room (#1). That leaves Onesimus reading Paul's letters in the scarlet room (#10).

ANSWERS

■

So the answers look like this:
Apphia, gray, singing
Archippus, brown, praying
Onesimus, scarlet, reading Paul's letters
Paul, purple, reading Old Testament
Philemon, white, reading the Gospels

Revelation
The Philadelphia church read from the book before the book read by the Ephesians (#11, Rev. 2:4). But Ephesus and Smyrna also read from back-to-back books (#2). So we must have back-to-back-to-back books, with Ephesus in the middle. Job-Psalms-Proverbs are the only books that fit that description. Since the psalm-readers enjoyed singing (#9) and the Proverbs people liked bowling (#1), we can fill in "Ephesus-Psalms-Singing" and "Smyrna-Proverbs-Bowling." We also know that the Philadelphians play word games, since the other P church (#4) was the Pergamum "white stone" church (Rev. 2:17) that spent its time sleeping. So we can fill in "Philadelphia-Job-Word games."

There are four books left. Genesis was read by another S church (#6), which must be Sardis. Joshua follows the word-game church, which we already know is Philadelphia, so that must be Laodicea. Thyatira "tolerated Jezebel" (Rev. 2:20) and thus did not read Isaiah, which leaves Jeremiah. By elimination, Pergamum read Isaiah. (And we already know they're the sleepers.) There are still three activities left, but we know that chariot races and dessert-eating were not done by the readers of Jeremiah (# 5), so that gives us "Thyatira-Jeremiah-Archery." Since the dessert-eaters' book follows the chariot-racers' book, we can pin it down to "Sardis-Genesis-Chariots" and "Laodicea-Joshua-Dessert."

The answers look like this:
Ephesus, Psalms, Singing
Smyrna, Proverbs, Bowling
Pergamum, Isaiah, Sleeping
Thyatira, Jeremiah, Archery
Sardis, Genesis, Chariot races
Philadelphia, Job, Word games
Laodicea, Joshua, Eating dessert

ANSWERS

SECTION 2

TRAVEL GAMES (pp. 78–96)
Soap Operas (p. 84)
1. Adam and Eve
2. Samson and Delilah
3. Mary and Joseph
4. David and Goliath
5. Ruth and Boaz

SECTION 3

FAMILY GAMES (pp. 98–111)
Mix-Up (p. 101)
1. David
2. Paul

3. Deborah
4. Isaiah
5. Elisha
6. Rahab
7. Moses
8. Timothy
9. Sarah
10. Matthew
11. Jacob
12. Reuben
13. Rebekah
14. Martha
15. Esther
16. Solomon
17. Samson
18. Barnabas

ANSWERS

Part Two: Fun for One

SECTION 1

WORD SEARCHES (pp. 116–167)

Water, Water Everywhere

Fear Itself

Sing a Song

Shophar, So Good

ANSWERS

Fire Away

Hide and Seek

Animal Tales

Pot of Gold

ANSWERS

Up a Tree

Bodies of Water

Acquainted with Angels

Kings

ANSWERS

Apostles

Women of the Bible

People Jesus Knew

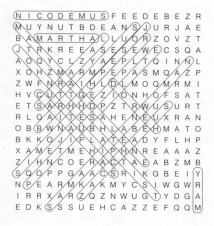

Books of the New Testament

ANSWERS

Beasts and Birds

What's for Dinner?

Bible Places

Books of the Old Testament

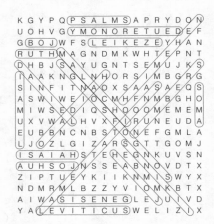

ANSWERS

Genesis

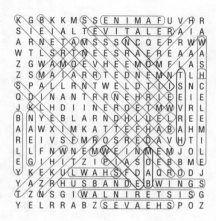

Ruth

Numbers

Elijah & Elisha (1 & 2 Kings)

ANSWERS

Life of David (1 Chronicles)

Proverbs

Job

Jonah

ANSWERS

Habakkuk

```
I R E G N I L T G N Q E W I N E H I
G N O T O X N D I K D D R I N K V M
A E C H Z E F A X T R T A K W E I A
L Y C E R T G I O V E N G J A R O G
L E E I N T R L S H A E E I B U L E
O D S C S S E A S K D L N S B T E W
P X O U C R E I M U E I O N D E L A
S R J A A O F Y K B D S T A E U C T
V N S T R A P M A R L H S I S V E E
U D E H O R D E S D B E H N P P X R
O E I B E N Q T S Y G S D O A L T S
C L P E R E G N A L E Z F L L E E T
H P G N I T S A L R E V E Y L O G E
E M K R O W D O O W J T W B O P A L
Z A S P M A R A Q H C E Z A C A R B
V R K P P T E N G A R D O B R R D A
C T G J E T I R W Y R A M B S D Z T
Z F F N P Q E L U C I D I R M S Y G
```

Matthew

```
R S W Z Y D M M X W Y M M D O T H P
F A M J S W R T H E E E A I F E G Z V
D B A O C U C E L D E G L G B B A U
E R A E G D U J P U I V R S L O P A M
R U G R D H D U T N A M H U T O O T O
G I O D I O A O H E A M B R L O I Z R
I I F U C A L A R G M A O D E E E T S
F M I N Y B R A S I N D E B N T C E O
S K P N B B B Y O S Q I E L E S E A F
N A R L A V E T N E I E S A S B E L Y
A R O S C A H I R A T X F S H E O C F
T S Q B D O V R P V W O E E H E L C O P
U T C E N T U R I O N E D Z Y X W L
T E V F C R U M B S P Y M H W A B B
A R D V N O T T U L G E S V L T R R
```

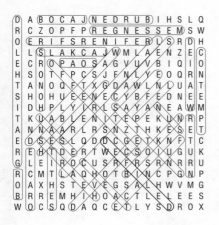

Malachi

```
D A B O C A J N E D R U B I H S L Q
R C Z O P F P R E G N E S S E M S W
O E R I F S R E N I F E B S R D H
L L S L A K C A J W M L A E N Z E C
E C R O P A O S A G V U V B I Q I O
H S O T F P C S J F N L Y E O Q R N
A N O Q F T X G D A W L N U A T E
S H O H U E E N E C Y B F E D N E M
I D H P L Y I R L S A Y A N E A W P
I T K U A B L E N I T E P E K U N R L
A N N A A R L R S N Z T H K E S E T
E D S E S L Q D D C G E T K N F T C
R E H T D E R T W E C S O I U G U K
G L E I R O C U S R F R S R N R U P
R C M T L A Q H O T B I N C P G N O
A X H S T E V E G S A L H W V M G
B R R E M H I H O A C T L E L E E S
W O C S Q D A Q C E T L Y S D R O X
```

John

```
L D E T P H Y Z Y F I R O L G J W Y
W R N D I S Z T M A L K Y P Y R E R E
T E I F E L Y E L O O P B K D I L S
U H W A M F R N L R Z H R L N F L U
R P P T U B A S I N D E V F A P H R
L E G H F W O R D W A B A C S U A R
E H H E R E T E P N O M I S U E L I
C S W R E D C L M N O K I G O H T E
O U D W O P E A S J I T D N R H S Y C
U O S F N S V U B A Z R O E E T T T
R O P L I X I K S G P K B K V I D E I
T G I I C Y N C S A I I B K V E E H O
Y W T E O G E E A E N L D A S I E W N
A P Y S D L Y H L R A D R A F E E H J
B M E E K N T M O T L Q L T T B I W
D X C W M O L R A B E A B R U E L I
D S A F U G F A E S U H C L A M E H
A Y D H S P D M S C K F H C P Q F E
```

279

ANSWERS

Romans

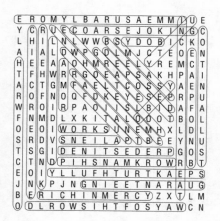

Titus

Ephesians

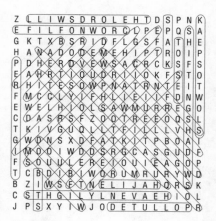

James

ANSWERS

SECTION 2

MATCHING (pp. 170–179)

Creation

1-d	5-c
2-g	6-f
3-b	7-e
4-a	

Events in the Life of . . .

1-c	7-a
2-l	8-f
3-h	9-e
4-k	10-d
5-b	11-g
6-i	12-j

Couples

1-k	8-h
2-e	9-l
3-m	10-g
4-b	11-d
5-f	12-a
6-c	13-j
7-i	

Parents and Children

1-f	8-h
2-e	9-c
3-n	10-l
4-b	11-d
5-a	12-k
6-m	13-j
7-g	14-i

Occupations

1-k	8-a
2-m	9-i
3-g	10-f
4-e	11-c
5-d	12-b
6-h	13-l
7-j	

Where, Oh, Where?

1-a	6-i
2-d	7-e
3-j	8-g
4-b	9-c
5-f	10-h

I Say to You

1-g	5-h
2-d	6-e
3-b	7-f
4-c	8-a

Brothers and Sisters

1-j	6-g
2-e	7-i
3-d	8-b
4-f	9-h
5-c	10-a

What Does It Say?

1-f	6-e
2-h	7-j
3-d	8-c
4-b	9-i
5-g	10-a

How Much?

1-g	6-e
2-c	7-f
3-a	8-b
4-i	9-j
5-h	10-d

HIDDEN WORDS (pp. 180–183)

#1 Ahimelech

Am, He, Ha, Him, Ham, Hem, Heel, Heal, I, Ice, Me, Ma, Mile, Male, Meal, Eel, Elm, Lime, Lame, Leech, Came, Claim, Camel

#2 Deborah

Do, Dab, Dare, Ear, Be, Bed, Bar, Bad, Bore, Bear, Bare, Boar, Beard, Oh, Or, Oar, Ore, Rob, Rod, Red, Rode, A, Ad, Are, He, Had, Her, Hard, Head, Hare, Hear, Heard

ANSWERS

#3 Matthew
Ma, Me, Mat, Maw, Mew, Met, Math,
Mate, Meat, Matte, A, At, Am, Awe,
Ate, Tam, Tat, The, Tame, Team,
Them, Thaw, That, Ha, He, Ham, Hat,
Hew, Hem, Heat, Hate, Eat, We, Wet,
What, Whet, Wham, Watt

#4 Jehoshaphat
Jet, Jot, Eat, East, He, Hat, Hot, Has,
Hop, Hoe, Hate, Heat, Hose, Hope,
Heap, Host, Haste, Oh, Opt, Oath,
So, Sat, Sap, She, Shop, Shah,
Shot, Shape, A, As, At, Apt, Ash, Pa,
Pat, Pot, Pet, Pest, Post, Past, Path,
Posh, Peat, Pose, Phase, Paste, To,
Toe, Top, Tap, The, Tape, Those

#5 Mesopotamia
Me, Mat, Map, Mom, Mop, Mate,
Moat, Mime, Mope, Moot, Mites,
Moist, Moose, Miasma, Eat, East,
Emit, So, Sat, Some, Same, Seam,
Seat, Soot, Soap, Oat, Omit, Pea,
Poi, Post, Pose, Poem, Pets, Peat,
Pots, Paste, Patio, Toe, Tap, Top,
Tip, Tame, Toes, Tempo, A, Am, At,
Aim, Ape, Atop, Atom, Atoms, I, It,
Is, Imp, Item

#6 Nebuchadnezzar
Need, Near, Ear, Earn, Be, Bar, Ban,
Bun, Bed, Bud, Bad, Buzz, Band,
Bane, Bare, Bear, Beer, Bead, Been,
Bunch, Beard, Bender, Buzzer,
Buzzard, Under, Car, Can, Cab, Cub,
Cad, Cud, Cube, Care, Czar, Char,
Cheer, Cherub, He, Ha, Her, Hand,
Hard, Head, Hear, Hare, Haze, A, An,
Ad, Are, And, Ace, Aced, Den, Dub,
Dun, Dare, Dear, Daze, Drab, Dance,
Dancer, Zebra, Red, Run, Rub, Rue,
Ran, Raze, Razz, Race, Read, Rend

#7 Apostles
A, At, Ate, Ape, Ale, Apt, Alp, Alps,
Apse, Alto, Also, Atop, Asset, Pa,

Pat, Pale, Pate, Peal, Pole, Post,
Pals, Peas, Plea, Pots, Pleas, Posts,
Postal, Plates, Opal, So, Sap, Sat,
Sop, Sot, Sea, Set, Seal, Seas, Sale,
Soap, Seat, Steal, Stole, Sepal,
Spate, Splat, Slept, Staple, To, Tap,
Top, Toe, Tea, Toes, Tale, Tape,
Teal, Tapes, Tales, Lo, Lap, Lop, Let,
Leap, Lope, Laps, Lost, Lest, Last,
Late, Less, Loss, Least, Lapse, Eat,
East

#8 Thessalonians
To, Tan, Tin, The, Than, Tail, Then,
Thin, Thai, Toss, Those, Talon,
Thine, Tassel, Tonsil, He, Ha, Hi,
Has, Hail, Hint, Hassle, Eat, Eon,
East, So, Sin, Sit, Sat, Sail, Sent,
Sass, Sole, Sins, Sons, Shone,
Shine, Snail, Stile, Stein, Stale,
Steal, Stones, A, At, As, An, Ash,
Ant, Ale, Ants, Alone, Asset, Lo, Lie,
Lit, Lot, Let, Lens, Lone, Loan, Line,
Less, Lion, Lasso, Lioness, Oh, On,
Oil, Oat, Oath, Onset, No, Not, Nil,
Nail, Nine, None, Note, I, In, Is, It,
Inn, Into, Inlet, Isles

#9 Revelation
Rev, Rat, Rot, Ran, Real, Reel, Rate,
Rail, Rain, Riot, Roil, Rove, Rave,
Rote, Rite, Roan, Rant, Rent, Ratio,
Revolt, Reveal, Ration, Relation, Eat,
Eon, Era, Eve, Ere, Eel, Ear, Earn,
Earl, Ever, Even, Evil, Elan, Event,
Elate, Elation, Elevator, Elevation,
Via, Veer, Veal, Vain, Vane, Vent,
Vote, Vine, Vile, Volt, Voter, Lo, Lie,
Lit, Let, Lot, Lore, Lair, Lain, Lion,
Leer, Love, Late, Lane, Line, Lone,
Lint, Lent, Lever, Laver, Lover, Liver,
Liner, Liter, Loner, Later, Latin,
Leaven, A, At, An, Are, Ale, Ant, Art,
Alto, Aver, Alit, Aril, Avert, Alien, To,
Toe, Tie, Tin, Tan, Ton, Ten, Tar, Tire,
Tare, Tore, Tone, Tine, Tale, Tail, Tile,
Tern, Torn, Toner, Tonal, Tailor, I, It,

ANSWERS

In, Ion, Ire, Into, Inter, Invert, On, Or, One, Ore, Oat, Oar, Over, Oval, Oven, Overt, No, Nor, Not, Net, Nail, Note, Never, Nerve, Native

#10 Bartholomew
Be, Bat, Bet, Bar, Bow, Boa, Bare, Bear, Bore, Boar, Boor, Boot, Boom, Bawl, Beat, Boat, Bowl, Boater, Boomer, A, At, Am, Awe, Ate, Art, Alb, Alto, Rat, Rot, Ram, Raw, Row, Rob, Rate, Roam, Robe, Real, Role, Robot, To, Toe, Too, Tea, Tar, Tab, Tow, The, Tame, Team, Tear, Tome, Tore, Tale, Them, Thaw, Tool, Term, Tower, Table, Throw, Threw, Tamer, Towel, He, Ha, Hoe, Hem, Ham, Her, Hat, Hot, Hew, How, Heat, Hate, Hobo, Howl, Harm, Hoot, Home, Hole, Heal, Heart, Homer, Oh, Or, Orb, Oat, Owl, Oar, Ore, Oath, Owlet, Other, Lo, Lab, Lot, Let, Law, Low, Lobe, Lore, Loot, Late, Loom, Lame, Lower, Looter, Loathe, Me, Ma, Mar, Mat, Maw, Mow, Mew, Met, Mob, Moot, Moat, Mole, Male, More, Moth, Math, Mower, Motor, Mother, Elm, Eat, Era, Elbow, We, Woe, War, Web, Wet, Were, Wore, Wool, Womb, Water

CRISSCROSS (pp. 184–191)
#1 Old Testament Characters

#2 Journeys of Paul

#3 Kings of Judah and Israel

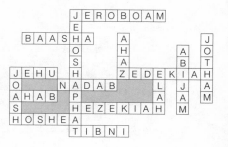

#4 Judges of Israel

ANSWERS

#5 New Testament Characters

#6 Tribes of Israel

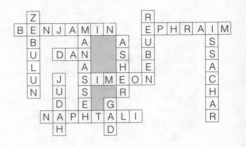

#7 Ephesians

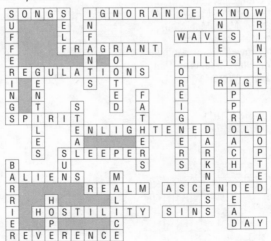

#8 1 Timothy

```
  S T R O N G       A B U S I V E
C         U         D           T E A C H
R A S H   A         A   C       E S     E
O         R     I M P O S T E R   I     R
P I E R C E D       N       N     A     A
S         E     H A S T Y   A     L     D
          M   P         C   L   D   D
A       I M M O R T A L I T Y
G A I N   O O           E   D P
E       D N P     A     E   E R
  W I N E   R   R C I V I L I A N
    N Y   I     U E     I U   V
A   G     E     U   S O L D I E R
B         T     M   L E D
A   E N J O Y M E N T   E
N V U       N   R   N S       M
D E D       T R U S T W O R T H Y
O   G       S   T   N         T
N E G L E C T       H         H
              E P H E S U S
```

ALPHAGRAPHS (pp. 192–195)

Flood Preparations

Ark, Believed, Construct, Destroyed, Endeavor, Form, Great, Help, Instructions, Join, Keel, Lip, Managed, Not, Only, People, Quickly, Rain, Soon, Though, Under, Very, Waters, eXhausted, Yet, Zebra

Beginnings

Adam, Beautiful, Created, Downfall, Eve('s), Forbidden Fruit, Good, However, Instead, Just, Kept, Let, Man, No, One, Parents, Quickly, Raised, Shepherd, Together, Until, Very, Wonder, X, Y, Zero

Down Time

After, Baal, Carmel, Depressed, Elijah, Flee, Godless, Heard, Incensed, Jezebel, King, Life, Mountain, Nothing, Over, Pity, Queen, Ready, Sat, Take, Utterly, Victory, What, eXasperated, You, Zealous, All, Broken, Calling, Death, Earthquake, Fire, Gentle, Here, Interested, Jealous, Knew, Listened, Murmuring, Now, Once, Powerful, Quietly, Realized, Still, Small, Told, Up, Via, Would, eXciting, Yes, Zest

CODES (pp. 196–198)

Code #1

Do not judge, and you will not be judged. Do not condemn, and you will not be condemned. Forgive, and you will be forgiven. Give, and it will be given to you (Luke 6:37-38).

Code #2

Shout for joy to the Lord, all the earth. Worship the Lord with gladness; come before him with joyful songs (Ps. 100:1-2).

Code #3

The stone the builders rejected has become the capstone; the Lord has done this, and it is marvelous in our eyes (Matt. 21:42).

ANSWERS

ALPHACODES (pp.199–203)

Verse A

Trust in the Lord with all your heart and lean not on your own understanding; in all your ways acknowledge him, and he will make your paths straight (Proverbs 3:5-6).

Verse B

Our Father, who art in Heaven, hallowed be thy name. Thy kingdom come, thy will be done, on earth as it is in Heaven. Give us this day our daily bread, and forgive us our trespasses as we forgive those who trespass against us. And lead us not into temptation, but deliver us from evil, for thine is the kingdom and the power and the glory forever and ever. Amen (Matthew 6:9-13).

Verse C

The parables of the hidden treasure and the pearl.

The kingdom of heaven is like treasure hidden in a field. When a man found it, he hid it again, and then in his joy went and sold all he had and bought that field.

Again, the kingdom of heaven is like a merchant looking for fine pearls. When he found one of great value, he went away and sold everything he had and bought it (Matthew 13:44-46).

Verse D

But when you give to the needy, do not let your left hand know what your right hand is doing, so that your giving may be in secret. Then your Father, who sees what is done in secret, will reward you (Matthew 6:3-4).

Verse E

I know what it is to be in need, and I know what it is to have plenty. I have learned the secret of being content in any and every situation . . . whether living in plenty or in want. I can do everything through him who gives me strength (Philippians 4:12-13).

Verse F

Beyond all question, the mystery of godliness is great: He appeared in a body, was vindicated by the Spirit, was seen by angels, was preached among the nations, was believed on in the world, was taken up in glory (1 Timothy 3:16).

MAZES (pp. 204–205)

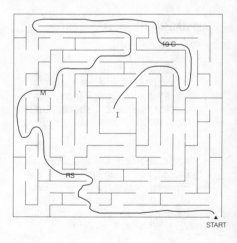

Wild Ones

ANSWERS

Christmas Shopping

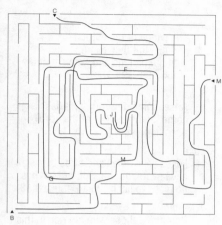

HANKY-PANKY (p. 206)
1. He saw Esau
2. Call Paul
3. Rude Jude
4. Hazardous Lazarus
5. Esther's jester
6. Adam had 'em
7. Moses poses
8. She be Phoebe
9. I lack Isaac
10. Noah's boa

RHYME TIME (p. 207)
1. Rahab; Ahab
2. Saul; Paul
3. Isaiah; Hosea
4. Cyrus; Jairus
5. Hezekiah; Jeremiah
6. Ishmael; Israel

WHERE IN THE BIBLE (pp. 208–212)
#1
Proverbs

#2
Matthew

#3
Isaiah

#4
Psalms

#5
Exodus

#6
Luke

#7
John

#8
Romans

#9
Daniel

#10
Esther

CHANGELINGS (pp. 213–214)
#1
MARK-MAKE-LAKE-LUKE

#2
LUKE-NUKE-JUNE-JUNO-JOHN

#3
JOHN-JOSH-JOTS-OATS-ACTS

#4
TRUST-UTTER-TREAT-HEART

#5
SINS-SONS-SNOW-SLOW-WOOL

PHONE FUN (p. 215)
1. "Everyone who calls on the name of the Lord will be saved" (Rom. 10:13).
2. "I love the Lord, for he heard my voice" (Ps. 116:1).

ANSWERS

3. "Pray for each other so that you may be healed" (James 5:16).

MYSTERY MATH (pp. 216–219)

#1
1 (5+2=7; 7+4=11; 11-8=3; 3-2=1)

#2
39 (10+12=22; 22-16=6; 6+40=46; 46-7=39)

#3
7 (27÷3=9; 9x2=18; 18+31=49; 49÷7=7)

#4
3 (969÷3=323; 323+7=330; 330-30=300; 300÷50=6; 6x2=12; 12+1=13; 13-10=3)

LINE-UPS (pp. 221–231)

Numbers
If the Lord is pleased with us, he will lead us into that land, a land flowing with milk and honey. (Num. 14:8)

Deuteronomy
Love the Lord your God with all your heart and with all your soul and with all your strength. (Deut. 6:5)

Ruth
We are witnesses. May the Lord make the woman who is coming into your home like Rachel and Leah. (Ruth 4:11)

2 Samuel
Oh, that someone would get me a drink of water from the well near the gate of Bethlehem! (2 Sam. 23:15)

1 Kings
Perhaps he is deep in thought, or busy, or traveling. Maybe he is sleeping and must be awakened. (1 Kings 18:27)

2 Chronicles
I have heard your prayer and have chosen this place for myself as a temple for sacrifices. (2 Chron. 7:12)

Job
The wings of the ostrich flap joyfully, but they cannot compare with the pinions and feathers of the stork. (Job 39:13)

Isaiah
Arise, shine, for your light has come, and the glory of the Lord rises upon you. (Isa. 60:1)

Luke
Foxes have holes and birds of the air have nests, but the Son of Man has no place to lay his head. (Luke 9:58)

1 Timothy
Command those who are rich in this present world not to be arrogant nor to put their hope in wealth. (1 Tim. 6:17)

2 John
And this is love: that we walk in obedience to his commands. As you have heard from the beginning, his command is that you walk in love. (2 John 6)

ANSWERS

Three Women

A	I	M			M	O	E
S	C	A	R		D	A	D	S
H	E	R	E		E	N	D	S
		A	B	A	B	Y	
		E	G	O		
		S	K	I	R	T	
A	S	I	A		A	R	E	A
R	U	T	H		H	E	E	L
T	E	E			E	L	L

Bible Books

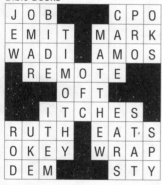

J	O	B			C	P	O
E	M	I	T		M	A	R	K
W	A	D	I		A	M	O	S
	R	E	M	O	T	E	
		O	F	T		
		I	T	C	H	E	S
R	U	T	H		E	A	T	S
O	K	E	Y		W	R	A	P
D	E	M			S	T	Y

Quotes

A	B	E	T		G	A	T	E
S	O	P	H		O	L	E	S
P	L	I	E		D	U	E	S
		C	L	A	I	M	S
		O	D	S		
	F	O	R	A	L	L	
B	E	N	D		O	A	T	S
S	E	M	I		V	I	A	L
A	D	E	S		E	D	G	Y

Stairway #1

```
I N
S O N G
  W O R D
    T O R N
      W A I L
        B L O T
          E V I L
            E D E N
              E G O S
                D O
```

Stairway #2

```
O N
F E A R
  T R A P
  T R E E
    E S A U
      O R N O
        S T A R
          O T I S
            H O O T
              N O
```

ANSWERS

Stairway #3